# Own Your
# AWKWARD

## LIFE CHANGES

the complete handbook for
## MASTERING CHANGE

## ANDY VARGO

Max —
Stay cool and
never change
what's in your
heart!
Andy

Own Your Awkward Life Changes

Text copyright © 2019 by Andy Vargo

All Rights Reserved

ISBN 9781077708808

Awkward Career Publications

awkwardcareer.com

# Praise for Own Your Awkward Life Changes

A while back, I introduced you to my friend Andy Vargo. He's a life coach and motivational speaker as well as the author of *Those Awkward One Drive Stands*, and the *Your Awkward Life* guided journal series. I'm so excited to share his latest book—hot off the presses—*Own Your Awkward Life Changes: The Complete Handbook for Mastering Change*. Vargo walks the reader through a unique system he developed to help us embrace change as a vehicle for growth rather than a source of angst and anxiety. From understanding the emotions of change to assessing resources and getting past roadblocks, this book will give you a more empowering perspective of change than you've ever had before.

One of the things I really appreciate about Andy is that he doesn't talk to you as a change expert on a lofty perch. He talks to you as someone who has experienced the anxiety of change the same way we all do, except he provides a painless pathway through it. The book is conversational in style and very easy to read and apply but loaded with substance.

Vargo's masterful storytelling combined with guided introspection and reflection worksheets transform an otherwise uncomfortable exercise into a journey of personal mastery and growth.

> Melissa Hughes PhD, Speaker and Author of Happy Hour with Einstein and Happier Hour with Einstein: Another Round

Finally, a lifeboat in the sea of never-ending-change! Own Your Awkward Life Changes: the Complete Handbook for Mastering Change provides powerful tools to help you quickly shift into taking constructive action to ensure a positive future, regardless of the situation you're facing. This book puts you back in the captain's seat of your own life.

Kimberly Davis, Author, Brave Leadership: Unleash Your Most Confident, Powerful and Authentic Self to Get the Results You Need

I thrive on change. Truly. I'm one of those people who stirs things up when I'm too comfortable and content. It has taken me decades to find productive ways to apply this characteristic, rather than suffer from it. By sharing these planning and adjustment strategies, Andy Vargo has created a great resource for me to use in my career and personal life. The best part? I have an additional resource to help others who don't have the same response to change that I do. Own Your Awkward Life Changes, reframes change as growth, which is a stroke of brilliance, because we know that mindset makes the difference in success or failure. Change is inevitable, wouldn't you prefer to make it your own, rather than have it forced on you? Read this book.

Sarah Elkins, Author of Your Stories Don't Define You, How You Tell Them Will, Storytelling Coach, Elkins Consulting Inc.

# Thank You

To those who have let me help you with the changes in your life. You have given me a gift I value more than I can express: your trust.

Thank you.

To my friends, new and old, who have laughed and cried with me through each of our own changes. You've made them all worth it with your gift: your companionship.

Thank you.

To my family for accepting the changes I have made in my life. You've given me a gift that has carried me through the darkest days: your love.

Thank you.

To my friends in the Plateau Area Writers Association who have been there through the changes in this book. Your gift has made me a better writer: your wisdom.

Thank you.

*"It is not the strongest of the species that survives, nor the most intelligent that survives. It is the one that is most adaptable to change."*

~Charles Darwin

# Foreword

One of the things I love about my life is getting to meet a lot of amazing people and even get to call some of them, friend.

Andy Vargo is one such individual. I've watched Andy's work for several years and we've had the opportunity to meet up over coffee. What I like about Andy is that while he is a skilled coach and thought leader he is also funny and relatable.

He also produces content that is funny, thoughtful, and inspiring. And that's how his book, *Own Your Awkward Life Changes,* is too. Reading it I felt as though I was sitting down having a chat with him.

When Andy asked me if I'd be willing to read his new book and write something up, I jumped at the chance to be one of the first to read it.

A book about managing change. Some people love change, some people hate it. But no matter how you feel about it, you will experience it because as they say, "Change is the only constant." That being the case, it makes sense to have a plan to navigate some of the bigger changes that we will face.

With something that affects us every day of our lives, you'd think we'd put more thought into our feelings about it. We may eagerly anticipate change and even work towards it or we might become frustrated with it and stew in our thoughts and feelings. But how many of us take the time to examine exactly how we feel about it?

This book should be a welcomed addition to the lives of anyone of any age.

Kids might be changing schools, their parents might be changing careers, and their parents might be changing from career to retirement.

Andy takes us through several steps in exploring our history of dealing with change and then introduces his *Mastering Life Changes system*.

With his charts and question-prompts we're asked to explore ways that a certain change might be positive and if there are any negatives to it, as well as how we might feel about it.

I have to say I'd never given much serious thought to the way I've handled change in the past. It's obviously a valuable exercise because as you probably know, past behavior can often predict future behavior.

This book directs us into a deep dive into what makes us tick regarding change. Many questions seem especially helpful: *Where do I create unneeded changes in order to avoid things I don't want to deal with? When have I missed out on adventures and promotions because I refused to make a change?* And many other great ones as well.

Something that I hadn't thought of before was that goals we set for ourselves are in fact, (desired) changes. And while it may be fun to dream about that home on the beach or the life of a digital nomad or even that perfect relationship, the reality of it can be difficult to bring together. And could bring with it stress, fear, and even negative consequences.

By utilizing the information and clear instructions in this book you'll also be prompted to explore some of those and to evaluate your *Assets and Resources*. And then, my favorite part, the *Navigation Map*.

Far too many people think that they have goals when what they really have are dreams. Goals without a plan and actions are just dreams.

Take the time to go through the process of the *Navigation Map*, exploring and completing the timeline, preparing for issues (things WILL go wrong). Then tackle those action steps, and I know you'll achieve your goals/changes easier and faster than ever before.

One of the unfortunate things about age is that many of us become more resistant to change. I think of the frustration I feel when I go into the grocery store and it's been remodeled. Things that I used to roll with easily have suddenly begun to bug me.

Perhaps the same as happened to you?

Darwin said that, "It is not the strongest of the species that survives, nor the most intelligent that survives. It is the one that is most adaptable to change."

I'm confident that with this book you and I can tackle changes, both negative and positive, more intelligently, more thoughtfully, and more effectively.

Read the book.

> Jim Kellner, CHt Certified Hypnotherapist, Tedx Speaker, and Leader of the *Damn I'm Pretty* movement

# Table of Contents

*"In any given moment we have two options: to step forward into growth or step back into safety."*

~Abraham Maslow

# Introduction

What enticed you to open this book? Are you ready to make serious changes in your life? Or perhaps life continues to change around you with little care for the direction you would like it to go. Regardless of why you are here, you have come to the right place.

While you may think of change as a four-letter word, it actually has six letters. Six letters, each representing one step of the process I teach in my coaching programs and I am going to share with you in this book.

However, there is a different six-letter word I like to use to replace the word change in order to begin the process of viewing changes in a positive light. And while this is never a welcome statement from someone thrusting change into their life, if you can take control and see it as such for yourself, it may be just the trick to shifting your perspective about change.

So what is this six-letter word?

Growth!

Change is the first step in achieving your own personal growth. As a human, change is the one constant thing in your life. From before you are born, you begin changing every minute. Some changes are more radical, more obvious, than others. Some are as subtle as the slow gentle movement of an incoming tide. Leaving you to suddenly notice that most of the beach is gone, taken from you inch by inch right before your very eyes.

But as much as you are changing every day, you are also growing. You cannot grow without changing. The opposite is also true: you cannot change without growing.

So if it seems difficult for you to embrace change, then perhaps you can embrace growth. Embrace the growth you will see by mastering the changes in your life.

How many times have you been told you need to learn to embrace change? How many of your bosses have said the changes coming are not a bad thing? How many nights have you sat up in bed, sick to your stomach, unable to sleep, because your mind is racing with how to deal with the life and career changes ahead?

If you are like me, then the answer to each of these questions is the same: countless.

I cannot tell you how many times I have rolled my eyes as the boss tells me I need to be ready to make adjustments for the changes headed my way. I have lost count of the number of nights I stayed up, thinking through any possible solution to get out of having to face the change thrown upon me, whether in my personal life or in my career.

If only I could go back in time to retrieve all of those wasted hours. If only I could relive those moments in order to spend that precious time focusing on making change work for me, rather than spending energy on the futile efforts to avoid the changes in my life.

I cannot go back in time, but I have broken the cycle for myself and have helped others do the same. Now, I can give you the chance to spare yourself the agony of a future full of uncertainty as to the outcome of the changes you face. Those answers are in this book.

In the pages ahead, you will learn the system I have developed to own the changes in your life. This is the process I walk my clients through step by step as they embark on the next leg of their own journeys. In this book you will learn the system at your own pace. You will explore your history of dealing with change, how you typically react, and learn how to apply this system in order to tackle the changes ahead with a focused mind.

Of course, no one can promise everything will go your way once you read a book. And of course, no one can claim to have a magic pill that will make all of your worries go away. However, as you learn the system in this book, you will give yourself the next best thing: empowerment.

Empowerment to take control of the direction your life is taking.

Empowerment to not feel lost in an ocean of life changes.

Empowerment to steer your life in the direction you want.

Empowerment to navigate the sea of change even in stormy waters.

## Before you begin:

Get the most out of your change journey by printing up free print-friendly versions of all forms and worksheets in this program by visiting awkwardcareer.com/change

*"The pessimist complains about the wind; the optimist expects it to change; the realist adjusts the sails."*

~William Arthur Ward

# An Ocean of Change

I've never been a good swimmer. When it comes to the idea of needing to sink or swim, I have always known I would find myself at the bottom of the sea with the pressure from a million pounds of water weighing me down. So when I found myself dropped into the torrent of ocean waves, tossing me like a ragdoll in every direction, I knew I had to find a way to survive. I needed to find my way to safer waters, or even better, the shore.

This is how the biggest change in my life hit me, all at once, caught off guard and unprepared.

Lost in a stormy sea of change, I had just told my wife of nineteen years I was gay, we were headed toward divorce, and life as I knew it was completely flipped upside down. My boat had capsized and I was thrown into stormy waters with no idea which direction to swim and no life boat in sight.

Change was happening, and I was grasping for anything that might float to help me get through it. I would not survive in this environment. I had to get back to shore, to regroup and feel safe before I could move forward.

Picture the ocean for yourself. Aside from the torrent I just described, many other images come to mind: a beautiful sunset, a vast overwhelming depth, stormy seas, the fear of the unknown, the gentle hush of waves rolling onto the beach on a sunny day. While you may think of the ocean in many different ways depending on your mood, the weather, or even the time of day, there is one thing that never changes about the ocean: it is always changing.

Unlike land which can stay the same with little noticeable change over time, the ocean is a moving life force changing wave by wave, moment by moment. The constant movement of the waves ensures nothing will stay still in this vast sea of change. If you drop a bottle into the ocean, it will begin moving the second it touches the water.

Using the ocean as a metaphor for change may leave you overwhelmed. You may feel you are there with me, tossed out of the boat, grasping for anything to get you to safety. It could seem the changes ahead are larger than you can handle. This is exactly how most of us typically feel with change. By using this example, I will show you that something you see as insurmountable, can actually be well managed, if you come at it with the right perspective and with a well-thought-out-plan.

Even in the midst of my turbulent waters, I knew if I could just get to solid ground, I could regroup and chart a course to take this life change in the direction I wanted and so desperately needed it to go.

In life, you, like the ocean are constantly experiencing change. Look back to the ocean you were picturing, but this time, place yourself on the edge of the shore. You are not yet in the middle of the changing sea. The shore represents your current state, your comfortable space.

Now, as you stand on the shore, looking out to the sea of uncertainty, be aware that you will be in the sea. Stormy weather or beautiful sunset, you will be in the thick of the ever-changing ocean soon enough. But the question is: In what way will you step into the water? To put it another way: How will change work its way into your life?

## Three types of change

Change happens in three ways.

The first way you experience change is like a changing tide. It slowly works its way in, as wave by wave it creeps closer and closer. Until finally, you are waist-deep in the changes you did not notice happening around you. Often times in this scenario, by the time you realize what has happened, the pull of the tide is overwhelming and you are forced to go with the flow whether you want to or not. When you finally notice that change has overtaken you, you feel surprised and betrayed, yet you are so thick in it that you have to just give in, or exhaust all of your energy fighting to stay on the shore which is now far behind you.

This type of change catches you off guard while deceptively allowing you to feel you are in your comfort zone. In a sense, the slowly rising tide forces your hand at one point along the way. You can buy into each wave of change as it slowly surrounds your feet. But sooner or later you must make a choice to go with the tide, or fight the pull as you work your way back to shore.

The hardest part of this change can be realizing it has happened and drawing a line in the sand as to where you will begin to take control and no longer let the current take you where it will. The more comfortable you become in any situation, the harder it becomes to stand up for your best interests. This is the trap with the slowly rising tide: by the time you understand the tone of the change, you have accepted the situation as your new normal.

Another way change takes over is much less subtle. It rolls in like the crashing waves of a tsunami taking immediate control of your life and leaving little care of subtlety or propriety. Changes like this, force you into immediate reaction. Typically, in this case, you do not take the best course of action. These are the times when you get to test your fight or flight responses. Unfortunately, whether you fight, flee, or freeze, it overwhelms you in the midst of a time when you need to be strategizing and implementing.

When change enters in this way, your first focus needs to be getting your bearings. The wrong choices will continue to be made until you slow down enough to consult your compass and determine which way to steer the rudder. If the waters refuse to settle, you must fight with all you have to get to calmer seas or even better solid shore. Once there, you can chart a course to navigate the changes towards the life you want.

The last and best way change can happen are the times you get to do just that: strategize and implement. In this case, you are back on the shore, on your solid ground once more. But in this case, you have time to plan for the changes ahead and pack your ship as you set out to sea with a map, a plan, and the supplies you need for the journey. This may seem rare, yet think of the times you had a goal you were working towards or a life change such as a move or job change you planned to make. In these times, you have had a chance to plan ahead, study the best options, and gather your supplies before you take the next steps.

This last example is your optimum position for approaching change. Although, as you know, you do not often have the luxury to be in the place you choose when it comes to dealing with the changes you face in life. This is where this book comes in.

The purpose of this book is to provide you with a manual to not only set yourself up as best as possible when you have the chance to be in your optimum position but to also help you identify where you are no matter the change scenario so that you may create your most optimum position from any point in the process.

The idea is to give you the tools for the process so at any point in your change journey, you can regroup and gain your footing in order to take control of the course and weather the changing tides of life.

When change hits you like the first two, a rising tide or a tsunami, you need to make your way towards the shore so you can place yourself in the optimum position to prepare for the rest of the voyage. This is how you take control of the changes in your life: by getting in position to plan where you will go moving forward. So whichever way change enters your life, get back to the shore to prepare for the rest of the journey on your terms.

Before you move on to understanding your relationship with change, take a moment to reflect on the change scenarios we discussed above, and think of a time in your life when you have experienced a change in one of each of the scenarios. Put some thought into each of the questions below. Write out a few sentences describing the situation, how you felt in the moment, and how you feel looking back.

Methods of Change

- When has change crept in like a changing tide?

  _____
  _____
  _____
  _____

- When has change taken over my life like a tsunami?

  _____
  _____
  _____
  _____

- When have I planned for a change that I wanted to make happen?

  _____
  _____
  _____
  _____

Having these answers front of mind will help as you dig deeper into better understanding you and your life changes. As you embark on your change voyage with your goals in view on the horizon, you will need to understand in what way this change has entered your life. By knowing this, you can identify whether you are ready to start planning or if you first need to get to safety before packing for the rest of the journey.

*"If you can't change it, change your attitude."*

~Maya Angelou

# Emotions of Change

*This doesn't make any sense,* I thought to myself as I sat in the parking lot, gathering the strength to turn the key and drive home for the last time ever. I had just been fired.

It wasn't getting fired that didn't make sense to me. I had been at odds with my boss since the day I started. Fellow employees shared that he had openly stated he didn't like the idea of hiring someone with more experience than him. I was doomed from the beginning.

No, losing this job made perfect sense. What didn't make sense to me was how I could be feeling so many contradictory emotions at the same time. If you asked me how I felt in that exact moment, I have no idea which emotion would have taken precedence. Within seconds, the winning emotion would shift from anger, to fear, finally to excitement, relief and happiness. Then again it would easily jump to a lack of confidence and sense of insecurity. And of course guilt. Guilt for not being able to provide for my family. Guilt for losing my job. Guilt for, in a way, being happy about it.

I had never been fired before. I did not know what to expect. This was an unwelcome change which I had not planned for. The one thing I did know was that I had bills to pay and three kids relying on me. I needed to mobilize quickly to find a way to earn income. If I were to let the emotions take control, I would be in a tailspin and this change would not go well.

I needed to pull the emotion out of the choices ahead. However, emotions can be motivating. How can you sort out when to let emotions play a part in moving you forward and when to keep them at bay? Emotions are in fact not a bad thing. Using them the wrong way is. Even worse is letting them use you.

If I were to let the emotion of anger take over my focus, I would be spending my energy on revenge, on proving myself in the right. I would not be spending time finding replacement income. If I were to let the feelings of freedom take control, I would be pushing aside the sense of urgency needed to take quick action. I would let things slide in my new justified reality.

Emotions have a place. They play an important role in your desire to make change happen. But their place is not in the captain's chair. In fact, their place is not anywhere on the bridge. They belong in the engine room, firing the engines, while your head stays clear to navigate the waters ahead. Think of it this way: emotions are fuel. Let them be the gas that runs your engine, not the wheel that steers your car.

The Mastering Change System is built around the logic of dealing with change. In this process, you will boil down the steps and the resources needed for you to take action and make your change a reality. The design takes the emotion from the decisions you will make regarding the changes you face. You cannot however, move forward if you do not first address and understand the emotions you feel.

I have been there. I have experienced change in many different forms. The changes I have faced have touched both my personal and professional lives. Imagine losing a job when you feel you are in the prime of your career, getting divorced and starting over at forty, coming out late in life, shifting your professional focus to leave your industry and start a new career with your own business.

Not all of my changes have been as crazy. I've dealt with promotions, a growing family, moving, and changing relationships. Some of these I handled well and am proud of. While others did not go so well, though these are the changes which taught me the greatest lessons.

Change is constant. You change every day at every moment. From subtle changes, you make without giving them thought such as shifting your body weight to ease discomfort, to more planned changes such as a retirement or wedding. Regardless of the change, your emotions come along for the ride. When you shift your body to be more comfortable, you feel at ease. When you plan for a wedding, you feel excitement, stress, happiness, and fear. These emotions could present themselves together, or at different times as you work your way through the timeline of your change.

Before you can dig deeper into the emotions of change I challenge you to open your mind in order to let go of some preconceived notions you harbor as to which emotions are tied to each change you face. You need to be able to view change as a neutral event, with emotions that come and go. Emotions which can be positive or negative at any given point.

In order to achieve this, you must first let go of the idea that changes are categorically bad or good. Changes in and of themselves are simply this, a change. You will not know until you work entirely through the change if that particular change brought results which were more positive or more negative.

You might, however, find yourself expecting a change to be bad or good as soon as you learn about it. Think of a few of the changes you have experienced in life. When you think back on these changes, did you expect them to be good or bad?

When you expect all good emotions to come from what you see as exciting changes, such as a wedding, promotion or new baby, you will feel confusion, guilt, and even depression, when emotions which do not seem justified surface. Though it is natural with any change to feel anxiety, fear, and many other less than desired feelings as you face a shift in your norm.

The same can be said for what you might otherwise categorize as a negative change. Let's look back at one of the hardest changes someone might face: job loss. Your initial thought may that be that this has to be a bad change. Initial feelings surfacing could be hurt, sadness, loss of confidence, and anger. But this is only looking at one slice of the timeline of this change. As you work through the job loss, these emotions may turn to feelings of freedom, excitement, empowerment, and happiness.

Let's look at facing a relationship change. Whether this is taking the next step in commitment, or choosing to end a long term relationship, many of the same emotions are at play. The key to understanding these emotions is being aware not all emotions will come into play at once. For example, you may experience feelings of fear, excitement, hurt, anger or a sense of relief throughout the process of this change. However, while you experience the fear or hurt, you may not be ready to feel the relief or excitement.

You see, at the beginning of the timeline you are only able to see your current position in the change model. However, as you work through the process your changes shift. While planning for a baby, you may feel excitement on day one, but then fear of your parenting ability as the event gets closer. With a job loss, you may feel scared you will not be able to afford food and shelter. This fear can shift to excitement when you find a new and possibly even better job.

It is very common to experience different feelings and emotions related to the same change depending on what stage of the change you are in. Something that may seem negative in the moment may block you from ever seeing any positive outcomes. In this way you may feel terrified or depressed while you work through a situation.

These emotions take over before you ever have the chance to feel relieved or excited about the new possibilities coming out of the change. The place you are in now and the strength of your emotions block you from seeing what you need to see.

This works both ways. In your excitement for the benefits you see in welcome changes, you can overlook things you would otherwise consider. You may move too fast and throw caution to the wind as you jump in with both feet. In this case, the excitement and happiness can be quickly washed away to disappointment and feelings of betrayal or lack of confidence as your rosy-eyed plan falls apart.

It is in this way you cannot label a change as good or bad carte blanche. You need to have time to experience the full process. Change is simply that, change. You may like some changes more than others, but at the end of the day it is your emotions, your perception, and your labelling, which determines if that particular change is one you see in a positive or negative light.

As you work through change, it is your job to steer the change in the direction you want to take your life. This is where owning change comes into play. This is when you take charge of your life. This is when you become empowered.

To truly understand the emotions of change, let's look at how they have played out as you have experienced a change in the past. First, let's look back to the emotions I experienced over the timeline after my job loss. Then you can walk through this exercise using an example of your own.

This exercise charts different emotions over the timeline of the change process. I have listed emotions I felt, and assigned a checkmark to note the strength of each emotion at different stages along the way. You will have a chance to create your chart in the upcoming pages.

My chart would look something like this example:

**Change:** Job Loss

|  | Emotion | Emotion | Emotion | Emotion | Emotion | Emotion |
|---|---|---|---|---|---|---|
| Stage | Happy | Sad | Freedom | Anxiety | Relief | Anger |
| Day 1 | √ | √√√√ | √√ | √√√√ | √√ | √√√√ |
| Day 30 | √√ | √√√ | √√√ | √√√ | √√√ | √√√ |
| Month 3 | √√√ | √√ | √√√√ | √ | √√√√ | √√ |
| Month 6 | √√√√ | √ | √√√√ | √ | √√√√ | √ |

As you can see in the example, I experienced levels of each emotion at different points along the course of the change. The end result of the change lies in your ability to guide the process without regard to your emotional state of mind in the moments you need to make critical decisions.

Negative emotions run strong. They come from out of the blue to punch you in the gut, leaving you breathless as you struggle to get to the next stage. Understanding their fleeting nature is critical to your success. You must be able to see the emotion for what it is: passing.

When dealing with the surprise attack of negative emotional breakdowns, one can be left feeling they are back at square one and starting over. Two weeks pass and you feel great the entire time. In your mind, you have gotten over the negativity. That is, until something triggers you, and all the pain and anger arise again.

Success is not the absence of emotion. Rather, it is the growing distance of time between emotional breakdowns. To this end, track the length of time between breakdowns. At the beginning of the process you might last an hour without crying. Later, you may be able to make it through an entire day. Before long, you may be up to a week, or even a month, without a relapse.

In this way, you are able to give the emotion time to pass before you step back into functioning at a higher level. You can say to yourself, *this is a tough moment, but I made it a month since the last one.* Once you let this pass, you can look forward to another month of progress. The danger is falling into the *back at square-one* trap. This is when you lose hope because you feel you have not progressed at all.

This can be equally damaging whether you are experiencing positive or negative emotions. If you feel hurt or anger, you could make choices out of spite and take actions that are vengeful and not serving your best interest. When you feel totally secure and excited about your prospects, you risk overlooking important questions and factors that need to be considered to protect yourself in the future.

You must see the notion of change as neutral, with the ability of different emotions to come and go as the process plays out. The purpose of understanding your changes in this way is to diffuse the power emotions play in your ability to cope with change and to make the right, and often tough, decisions you will need to make during this process.

Now take a moment to fill out the worksheet on the next page for yourself, reflecting on a change from your past:

**Change:** _____

|  | Emotion | Emotion | Emotion | Emotion | Emotion | Emotion |
|---|---|---|---|---|---|---|
| Stage |  |  |  |  |  |  |
| Day 1 |  |  |  |  |  |  |
| Day 30 |  |  |  |  |  |  |
| Month 3 |  |  |  |  |  |  |
| Month 6 |  |  |  |  |  |  |

As you see for yourself, each emotion shifts in its strength as time unfolds. Though each present differently, the root causes and feelings stem from your own unique set of experiences leading up to the change, coupled with the tools you are equipped with to handle the changes thrown into your life.

The Mastering Life Changes System is a very logical way to work through each element of facing change in your life. In order to make full use of this system you must understand the emotions of change. When you truly understand which emotions are at play, and how to reframe them, you can take them out of the conversation when it relates to making the tough choices ahead in order to move your life forward.

*"The curious paradox is that when I accept myself just as I am, then I can change."*

~Carl Rogers

## Acceptance of Change

If understanding the emotions of change is step one, then right behind that is acceptance. Acceptance of the change you are facing. Acceptance of how you feel about it. And acceptance of what you do and do not have control over.

Change is something you just have to accept. It does not mean you have to completely accept the result. However, you must be wise enough to understand which things are within your control to change, and those which are not. Those things which are outside of your control to change must be accepted before you can move forward.

At the beginning of my job loss, I did not want to accept that I did not have a job. But any time I spent fighting this idea, was time not spent on moving forward. In essence, the longer it took me to accept the situation, the longer it would take in order to control and steer the circumstances to a better place.

I had a choice. I could fight whether or not this change had happened, or should have happened. Or I could spend that same energy on creating a new life after the change. Any energy and focus

31

spent on one, comes out of the energy that I would need to focus on the other. In other words, you cannot move on as long as you are fighting to stay in the same place.

Once you understand the importance of acceptance, you can look at the changes you face and understand that the sooner you accept them, the faster you can recover. In a way, quickly accepting change becomes a race to recovery.

But how do you come to acceptance when there are aspects of change you know you do not need to accept? After all, if you want to create the life you want, you have to be willing to not accept the status quo. While this is true, the wisdom comes in not wasting time refusing to accept those things we have no control to change. This way of thinking will free up your mind to focus on that which you can change.

In order do this, you need to sort through what aspects of the current change you have the power to act on and what elements are out of your control. Spending energy on those things which are out of your control raises your stress level, distracts you from the actions you need to take and slows down your overall ability to move on.

To accomplish this, you need to work through each of the elements of change that may be weighing on your mind. This is best done by creating a list of each aspect of the change. In the upcoming exercise you will create a list of everything on your mind as it relates to the change you are facing. In a sense, you are writing out your *gripe* list. Then, you will reflect on each item on your list to determine if you have control of that element or not.

Once you have written your list and determined which items you have control over, and which you do not, you will write down what actions you can take to steer this change towards your best desired outcome. For any item you cannot control, write *'accept it and move on.'* For all other aspects, write down any action you can think of which you can take.

By looking at the elements of my job loss, my chart would look something like the example below:

**Change:** Job Loss

| Element of this change: | Control: | What I can do about it: |
|---|---|---|
| Lost my job | No | Accept it and move on |
| Lost source of income | Yes | Apply for new job<br>Do temp work |
| Too much time at home | Yes | Go to library to fill out applications |
| Missing work connections | Yes | Join new networking group<br>Schedule coffee meetings |
| Not enough qualifications for new positions | Yes | Take classes online<br>Consider other options |
| Disagree with reason for being let go | Yes/No | Fight the event, or Accept it and move on |

By writing these out, you spend time sorting out what it is that bothers you specifically, rather than getting caught up in your gripes about change in general. Once you write that you will *accept it and move on*, you give yourself permission to stop wasting energy holding on to the hope that you can fight to keep what is already in the past.

With my job loss, I had elements I was not happy about: not having a job, the loss of income, the way it was handled, and the reason given for being let go. With each of these I needed to determine if I had any control over the scenario in order to decide if I would stay preoccupied with my feelings, or if I would, in fact, accept it and move on.

One element I needed to make a choice regarding was my feelings for the reason in which I was let go. While the choice they made and the reasoning they used to come to their decision was out of my control, whether or not to fight my case was within my control. At this point I needed to make a decision whether it was in my best interest to fight for the job, or to accept it and move on.

Fighting my case would mean I could possibly receive compensation for lost wages. Even closer to home, a win would mean some sense of repair to my damaged ego. However, taking this route would also be a risk as there would be no guarantee I would win. At the same time, the energy I would spend proving my side would be time and attention I would not be giving to searching for a new job.

Accepting the situation as it was and moving on would mean all of my efforts could be put towards finding replacement income. Whether this was through taking courses to increase my qualifications, going to networking events, or spending time seeking out and applying for new jobs. I chose to accept it and move on.

I call out this example, because it is important to acknowledge that even some things which we may have some control to hang on to are not in our best interest to do so. And even if it is not the only choice, we do have the choice to accept it and move on.

In the chart on the next page, start in the first column by identifying each of the elements of the change you are facing. This is where you list any way in which this change has impacted you. Then note in the second column whether this aspect is within your control or not. The last column is for you to decide what action you have control to take in order to deal with each piece of this change. For any element you cannot control, write: *'accept it and move on.'*

Change: _____

| Element of this change: | Control: | What I can do about it: |
|---|---|---|
| | | |
| | | |
| | | |
| | | |
| | | |
| | | |
| | | |
| | | |
| | | |
| | | |
| | | |
| | | |
| | | |
| | | |
| | | |
| | | |

Change is going to happen in your life. Your success in dealing with change comes first from the speed of your ability to adapt to a new reality in the midst of each change you experience. The longer it takes for you to accept that change is happening or has happened, the longer it will be before you can take the actions needed to create your new reality. Creating a list will help you look rationally at what your mind and emotions may be working through.

*"The only way to make sense out of change is to plunge into it, move with it, and join the dance."*

~Alan Watts

## Change Relationship

*If I am ever going to pursue my dream, it has to be now.* I've now lost my job, am divorced, and out living my authentic life. Now is the time to start building my career to be in line with something I am passionate about.

When I started this career change, I had learned more about myself, though I still had much to learn as to my relationship with change. I had learned that I need to *slow my roll,* if you will. My first instinct with change is to jump right in. This can serve me well when a quick reaction is needed, but when larger things are at stake it can greatly undermine the possibility for good results.

I had learned that I need to stop, think, and then proceed in order to take time to put a plan in place that will capture all of the opportunity ahead. So, when it came to start my business and go full time as a writer and speaker, I was able to start applying what I had been learning about myself.

I had learned not just about my emotions of change, but also better understood my relationship with change. Fixing anything in our lives first comes down to understanding what our relationship is with that very thing. You cannot eat healthier, if you do not have a grasp of your relationship with food. How and when do you use it to cope with life, and when do you use it to celebrate? This was a discovery I needed to make for myself with regards to change.

Having a better understanding of my instincts and desires, sets me up to know when these work for me, and when they do not serve me well. Admittedly, some days were tough. I was ready to take action. I wanted to jump right in and get the word out before I had finished my full marketing plan. But I was beginning to understand this as an instinctive move on my part which does not work for my best interests. Fighting this instinct was, and honestly still is, a constant battle.

In this section, you will find an understanding of your relationship with change by taking the Change Relationship Assessment at the end of the chapter. As you work through each aspect of your current relationship, there exist questions you will need to ask yourself and be honest about. This is not a time to answer based on the ideal answer, but rather to have that tough reality check with yourself.

Answering honestly will give you a true assessment of where you are coming from. It is only then, you can understand where you are as it relates to your relationship with change. Without knowing, and fully understanding this position, you cannot take the first steps in your change journey.

To put it another way, if you want to sail to Mexico, you first need to know which port you will depart from. Your plan will be different if you live in New York, Seattle, or Brazil. How else will you know where to plot your course and in what direction to set sail?

Often times, this is the first critical mistake people make in dealing with change: not slowing down enough to understand where they are in the first place. Your first instinct is to take action, to get out of where you are, to make a change just for the sake of seeing a difference. However, without taking a careful and honest assessment of your current surroundings, you wind up in a new place but with all the same issues and feelings of frustration and disorientation you felt before you left.

Have you ever made what you thought would be a life-altering change only to feel like everything is the same after all of the dust settles? How do you feel when all of your efforts land you back in the same place? These situations occur when you do not fully understand your relationship with change and how to use it to your benefit.

With that in mind take a few minutes to reflect on the upcoming questions. You can answer them in the lines provided at the end of this section, or use your journal for more space. Taking time to work through the assessment is the foundation of fully understanding how you can be best equipped for the voyage ahead.

As you work through this assessment, you will find that the questions are broken into two categories: welcome changes and unexpected changes. I have chosen these labels specifically to reinforce the idea that change in and of itself is neutral. You react differently if it catches you off guard, or if you feel it is in line with your plans for life. Thus the terms of welcome or unexpected rather than positive and negative.

*How do I deal with change?*

This is a complex question. Everyone deals with change in their own unique way. To complicate matters even further, we each deal with different types of changes in varying ways. This is split into two separate questions. The first being: how do I deal with welcome changes? The second being: How do I deal with unexpected changes?

Ask yourself the following questions as it relates to each type of change:

- When do I jump in with both feet?
- In what ways do I bury my head in the sand?
- When do I brush it off and avoid dealing with it?
- How do I take charge and try to control every step of the way?

- When do I avoid responsibility by letting things *take their course?*
- How do I allow the circumstances to dictate how this will play out?

As you can imagine there are pros and cons to how you deal with even the welcome changes in your life. Just because you are facing a change for the better does not mean you are navigating it in the best way. You can still pull the wrong tools out of your tool-bag: over-controlling, lack of planning, or unrealistic expectations just to name a few.

By taking time to reflect on your pattern of coping with change, you will become aware of your go-to methods. This is critical to understand so you can learn when to use these to your benefit as well as when to reign them in to protect yourself from becoming your own worst enemy.

## How do I feel about change?

Honestly, how do you really feel? You should have a better understanding of this after reflecting on the previous chapter. Take a moment to reflect on your chart of emotions and ask yourself which emotions first came to mind when you think about change.

Even otherwise welcome changes can bring negative emotions. Let's pretend for a moment the change you face will be a promotion at work. On the surface, this is a positive change. You might reflect on the excitement of moving forward in your career or the relief of receiving a pay raise. However, along with those positive feelings can come the fear of how you will perform, or how your peers will accept you in your new position.

On the other side of the coin are the reactions you feel to unexpected changes such as a job loss. You could fear for your security and perhaps have a loss of confidence in your abilities. Yet you might also have surprisingly positive emotions such as relief from the stress and pressures of work. These may then be followed up with guilt for having any good feelings in a time you expect to be negative.

Consider these thoughts when answering this question:

- In what way am I reacting to an expected outcome from change?
- Which fears are fueling my emotions during this change?
- Which hopes are leading my positive emotions?
- Which experiences from my past are distorting my view of the current changes in my life?

The emotions you bring into this change are a result of how well you have handled your changes in the past combined with the similarities you see in your current situation. This can serve you well when you need to be warned of danger so you do not continually make the same mistake. Think of hearing a smoke detector and knowing there is potential for a fire. However, without understanding your emotions and fears and what they are based in, you will not know if they are protecting you or holding you back.

*What are the instinctive actions I take when facing change?*

Change, whether welcome or unexpected awakens your natural instincts. Before you have time for your conscious brain to work and logical thought to kick in, your first instincts take precedence. Your fight or flight instincts surface based on the emotions that awake in the face of change.

These emotions may be different whether you view the upcoming change as a threat or an opportunity. Either way, taking action without understanding your motives, strengths, and weaknesses, will produce less than optimum results. Possibly even disasters.

A few questions to ask yourself:

- Do I typically do the same thing in the face of change?
- Do I over-analyze it? If so, in what ways?
- Do I jump in without thinking everything through?
- Do I get paralyzed with the fear of things not going my way?
- Who do I complain to about aspects of change?
- Do I create drama until no one wants to be around me?

- With unexpected changes, how do I avoid jumping in so that I do not have to face my fears?
- With positive changes, when do I jump right in without taking the time to prepare?

Your approach to each change will be different based on your perception. In essence, you are stepping into your first actions with your own bias as to how you expect this change to go. Your perception of the situation and your feelings surrounding it dictate your first instincts when facing change. Understanding what these are and how they play out will help you take control of the process and make sound choices with your best interests in mind.

### How do I use change to deal with life?

Your view of change may typically be seen as something that simply *happens* in your life or that *happens* to you. Yet throughout the course of your day, you constantly use change to deal with your surroundings. You can act as though you do not like change, yet as with so many other coping mechanisms, you are more than happy to pull change out when it suits you.

Think about things as simple as being in a public place. When something changes to make the atmosphere less comfortable, do you get up and leave? The mood shifts. Perhaps a conversation nearby makes you feel uncomfortable, the music gets too loud, or you begin to feel unsafe. Most likely in these scenarios, you will relocate. You make a change.

This may not sound all that groundbreaking, or unreasonable. But what about the big issues you make changes to avoid? What about the relationships you cut off, the jobs you leave, or the opportunities you miss when you either change to avoid them or refuse to change to let them happen? In each of these instances, you are making choices to use change to stay in your comfort zone.

When it comes to answering this question, keep these ideas in mind:

- When have I missed out on adventures and promotions because I refused to make a change?
- What great relationships have I lost because I was afraid to face changes?
- When have I made a preemptive change in order to avoid the chance of things being out of my control?
- Where do I create unneeded changes in order to avoid things I do not want to deal with?
- How can creating change be a coping strategy for me?

Whether you admit it or not, you are already using change daily to fit your needs. You simply pick and choose when to label this as a good thing or a bad thing. By looking honestly at your behaviors, you can step into the Master Life Changes System, knowing when to use these behaviors to your advantage and when to make sure to keep them under control.

### What has been my history of results from change?

For a host of reasons which we will not be able to address within the pages of this book, it is too easy to self-sabotage yourself when facing change. Creating a complex dynamic that goes far beyond the simple notion that welcome changes will go well and unexpected changes will end in disaster.

Many of us are the type who thrive in crisis mode. Yet when things are going well, we simply botch the landing, for lack of a better term. So when looking at this question, you must sort the differences in your performance and tendencies between welcome changes and the tougher unexpected changes you face.

Reflecting on this question, here are a few things to ask yourself:

- What is my history of knocking life changes out of the park?
- How do my results vary between personal and career changes?
- Which types of change do I handle best? Worst?
- How quickly do I mobilize to face negative changes?
- How well do I prepare to make the most out of positive changes?

Results serve as evidence and often a precursor to your future success. Taking a look at your past results is not for the purpose of continuing the same course. Nor is it to wallow in defeatist ideas. Rather, take this step in order to understand the areas where your current strategy is working and where it is not. By having a better grasp of what works to your benefit and what holds you back, you can look at the behaviors which create those results.

Once you are empowered with this understanding, you can make choices to steer your behavior in the direction you intend to take your life. You can look back at the past to find patterns in order to learn where you struggle and where you shine. This is true empowerment. This is where you get to make the choice whether the destination will, in fact, be fruitful, or a chance to learn from less than stellar results.

### Which life changes have I dealt with the best?

Whether or not you give yourself credit, you have done some things well in your life. These might come to mind right away: that time you moved and everything fit perfectly in the truck. You may need to rack your brain to go back through everything you have dealt with and overcome in order to find something you feel worked out the way you wished. Regardless, those times are there.

Those times worked out for you and there are reasons why. You stepped into the change with a different mindset. You were more prepared. Perhaps you were more open to a flexible course of action. Whatever the reason, you made the change happen for your benefit.

Beyond just the one-word answers as to what the event was, consider the circumstances of each change. Get to the details of the pattern in order to understand what your motivations and fears are. This will prove helpful in protecting yourself from self-destructive tendencies in order to be ready to make the most out of the change you now face.

When reflecting on which life change you have dealt with best and what you did well, dig deep with these questions:

- What was the scenario?

- What was the tide of the change? Welcome or unexpected?
- What did I do differently in this change than with others?
- How was I positioned stepping into this change?
- In which way did this change occur?
- What lessons did I learn that I can keep with me?

Keeping these thoughts front of mind as you move forward with your next goal will reinforce the idea that you can make change work for you. This positive mindset will power the momentum you need to work through the hurdles you will encounter along the way.

Come back to this question when you need a boost. Sometimes you just need to remind yourself what you have accomplished and what works for you in order to face the obstacles ahead with confidence.

### Which changes were the worst and hardest for me?

Not only do you need to look at the best times in your life, but more importantly you also need to give a good, hard look at those which did not go so well.

It is in these events you can learn your biggest lessons. Your disastrous failures often become the most valuable times in your life. That is, if you learn from them. The lessons you take from your failures and disappointments set you on a course for future success. As you look at these times in your life, focus on letting go of the emotions surrounding the event in order to see what behaviors were at play.

Give some thought to the entire situation as you reflect on the questions below. Be as hard on yourself as you need to be, while still giving yourself credit for what you did well.

- What was the scenario?
- What was the tide of the change? Welcome or unexpected?
- What did I do differently in this change?
- How was I positioned stepping into this change?
- In which way did this change occur?
- What lessons did I learn in this change that I can keep with me?

Each change, whether it went well or not, has elements of success and failure. You may look at a time in your life when you can see where you started managing a situation well, but then lost your stamina and let things fall to the wayside. Or you may have experienced a change which started as a complete mess, but you managed to pull it together. Both changes seemed on a set course, had your actions not intervened.

Looking objectively at your history, you can set yourself up for future success. Do this by finding your own weaknesses and blind spots. This will set you up to step into future changes aware of where you need to be the most diligent in order to not drop the ball.

*Change Assessment*

With these thoughts in mind, take a moment to work through each aspect of the Mastering Change Assessment on the following pages:

# MASTERING CHANGE: ASSESSMENT

Take this assessment to form your foundation.

How do I feel about welcome changes?

_____

_____

How do I feel about unexpected changes?

_____

_____

How do I deal with welcome changes?

_____

_____

How do I deal with unexpected changes?

_____

_____

Which actions are my first instinct when facing welcome change?

_____

_____

Which actions are my first instinct when facing unexpected change?

_____

_____

What is the typical result from how I handle welcome changes?

_____

_____

# MASTERING CHANGE: ASSESSMENT

Take this assessment to form your foundation.

What is the typical result from how I handle unexpected changes?

_____

_____

Which life changes have I handled the best?

_____

_____

What did I do well during these changes?

_____

_____

Which life changes were the worst or most challenging for me?

_____

_____

What didn't I do well during these changes?

_____

_____

How do I use change to cope or avoid issues in life?

_____

_____

How have I used changes to my advantage in the past?

_____

_____

Did you learn anything new about yourself? I know I sure did. This is an exercise I come back to from time to time, after experiencing more life changes. I find as my relationship with change evolves I continue to have new lessons. New habits form, old habits resurface.

In any relationship, you must understand how you play a part in the equation. Change is no different. It will continue to evolve as you grow. Keep these questions in mind as you work through the next steps of the process. Refer back from time to time in order to check in on your relationship with change.

*"They always say time changes things, but you actually have to change them yourself."*

~Andy Warhol

# The Mastering Life Changes System

So what exactly are we getting into? If you are like me, nothing leads me on more than a book which promises solutions and ideas but never clearly states what to expect or how we will get there. Let's get that out of the way right here.

The Mastering Life Changes System is a very simple series of worksheets you will reflect on and answer throughout each chapter of this book. Each section focuses on a different aspect of the C.H.A.N.G.E. System outlined below:

**C**learly Identify Change/Goal

**H**onest Budget

**A**ssets & Resources

**N**avigation Map

**G**etting Past Roadblocks

**E**valuate & Evolve

In a nutshell, you will learn to make things happen from beginning to end. Starting with organizing your thoughts around the changes you are facing, working through challenges and roadblocks, and finishing up with evaluating and evolving as your change is realized.

This overview will give you an idea of what to expect in this system. Each section will focus on a different element you will be learning and putting into place.

There are so many variables to the changes in your life. How can you develop one way to deal with anything that comes your way regardless of the situation? You do this by getting to the root fears and emotions that most often hold you back from dealing with change successfully. By focusing on your perspective of how to deal with situations, you diffuse the emotional bomb held over you. This allows you to think clearly and more readily use the resources at hand.

Each step of the way is outlined following the C.H.A.N.G.E. System as explained here:

## Clearly Identify Change

Before you can understand how to deal with the changes in your life, you must have an idea of where you want to go. This step walks you through a series of questions to think through in order to gain a clear idea of your best-desired outcome. This will answer your *why* as it relates to the change you are facing.

## Honest Budget

Step two is all about understanding what you have to work with. When you face changes, it is easy to get caught off guard with a lack of resources. This can often be avoided if you take the time to allocate the resources you have in a way that supports your goals. In this step, you do just that. This process will walk you through your three most valuable resources: money, time, and energy.

## Assets & Resources

Having taken a look at how and where you allocate your budget, step three digs deeper into compiling a master guide to every asset and resource you have at your disposal. You have more help available than you realize. Compiling a master list of who and what can be of assistance will empower you to manage the changes in your life.

## Navigation Map

Now and only now can you begin to map your way through the changes you are about to face. By the time you get to step four, you will have a clear understanding of where you are, where you want to be, and what you can use to get there. Essentially your ship is now loaded and ready to depart. Before you take any action though, you must have a map to be sure you are headed in the right direction. This step brings that map to life.

## Getting Past Roadblocks

But what happens when things don't go to plan? You can lay out the best map and know exactly where you plan to go. But then you inevitably reach an impasse. However, things not going to plan is what life is all about. It is the reason you are here in the pages of this book right now. Knowing there will be challenges and detours is all part of the process. Planning ahead to get around them is the difference which will have you mastering your life changes.

## Evaluate & Evolve

You might not like to hear this, but the last step of the C.H.A.N.G.E. System is in fact, more change. As you know, the one constant in life is change. So you too must understand how to view your change as an evolving opportunity to better yourself and your position in life. This step will identify where you are and what adjustments you may wish to make along the way.

If this system sounds simple, that's because it is. One of the worst things you can do in the midst of change is to overcomplicate things. This system is designed to keep your focus on the task at hand without getting caught up in all the what-if scenarios. You are facing change, you need to take action. You need to take control of your life. There is no time to waste on anything beyond the task at hand.

## MASTERING LIFE CHANGES

Change is the one thing we can count on always being consistent. Like it or not we will always have to deal with changes in life, both in our personal lives as well as our careers. The sooner we learn the tools to master life changes, the better we will be for the rest of our life. Using this Six-Step Mastering Life Changes System, you will be prepared to manage the changes that you can be sure life has in store for you.

Six-Step Mastering Change System:

**C**learly Identify Change/Goal

**H**onest Budget

**A**ssets & Resources

**N**avigation Map

**G**etting Past Roadblocks

**E**valuate & Evolve

*"There are far better things ahead than any we leave behind."*

~C.S. Lewis

# Clearly Identify Change or Goal

Before you can put your plan in place, you have to know just where you are going. Now that you have completed the Change Relationship Assessment, you have a better understanding of how you use changes and perhaps even how you are used by changes when you are not in control of them.

Knowing this, you can start to look at the changes you face now. Step one is to clearly identify your change or goal. A goal is nothing more than change with a direction in mind. For the purpose of clarity, I like to remind people that achieving their goals is nothing more than making the changes happen that you want to see in your life.

So with that in mind, where do you even want to go? This is the first thing you need to decide. When I was young I thought it didn't matter. I thought I could explore life and just make those decisions along the way. And while that is not bad in and of itself, there is no guarantee of it taking you to any special destination. You could have some great experiences along the way, and you may land somewhere you want to be, but you will always be at the mercy of chance.

While there are times in life when leaving it up to chance is perfectly acceptable and appropriate, it leaves you powerless in directing your own course. I imagine if you are in one of these times, you would not have picked up this book, to begin with. So let's make the assumption that you are in the mindset to be ready to take control of your life and chart a course towards the change, or goal, you want to make happen.

Step one in this process is simply identifying what you are dealing with, and where you want to go. You must understand a few things. You must know where you want to end up. How can you pack for a trip if you do not know the destination? Preparing for a trip to Antarctica is much different than packing a bag for Hawaii.

Not only must you know where you want to end up, but you need to also know where you currently are in the process. When you get in the car and head down the road, you need to know if you must drive north or south.

If you do not first know where you want to go, and where you are in relation to that place, then you will remain lost. You will keep driving in circles, hoping to accidentally stumble upon the hidden doorway to your dream life.

The following worksheet will walk you through a series of questions to think through in order to identify your change or goal. I interchange these words in this step as realizing a goal you have would, in fact, be a big change for you. Mastering change is accomplishing goals, and if we accomplish goals we are in effect mastering a life change.

Let's look at some things to consider when answering each of the questions on the worksheet.

### Who does this change affect?

This may seem like a simple answer: you. But in life, anything you change about yourself will have a ripple effect, good or bad, to those around you. It is, in fact, impossible to make changes in your own life without having those changes touch others.

When you think through this question, try to look at it from as many different angles as possible.

Some things to consider:

- How could this change affect the relationships I have?
- Which relationships might need to end?
- Which relationships will get stronger or closer?
- How might people nearby react to me with this change realized?
- How will I be more or less available to those around me?
- In what way will I be able to help my friends more? Less?

To think that you are the only one affected by the choices you make in your life can be a closed-minded and selfish way of looking at it. You must consider all of the players in order to truly, clearly identify your goal.

### *What is the best desired outcome from this change?*

Depending on the change you are making, this may not be so straight forward. For example, let's say your change is to advance your career. In order to understand this change the best, picture the outcome beyond just getting that promotion. You must picture what your life will look like when this change is realized. When all is said and done, will you be living the lifestyle you want?

Be sure to consider the ways in which reaching this goal will affect your life. Ask yourself questions such as:

- What do I want my life to be like after this change is complete?
- Who will I be spending the most time with when I am through?
- What will my finances look like?
- Will I have more or less time to spend with family? On hobbies?

By considering the big picture of what you desire, you can fully understand if this is the right change to make in order to create the life you want.

*When do I need to be through with the changes I am facing?*

On the surface, this seems to be a much more to the point question. Depending on the type of change you are facing, you may know an exact hard deadline that is non-negotiable.

For example, if the change you face is adding a member to your family, and a baby is already on the way, then you have no wiggle room to make that happen. Or if you have lost your job and have a limited amount of time before your funds dry up, then you know your change must be completed by then.

However, there are times when you can become impatient for change, and by slowing down to ask yourself when you really do need the change to be done, you can better understand when to push harder. You can also see when you should give yourself the grace to slow down to get your bearings before you push through the stormy sea of life.

Consider these questions:

- Is the deadline I have non-negotiable?
- Which aspects of the change need to be done sooner than later?
- What are the consequences of not meeting the deadline?
- What consequences will come from rushing to meet a deadline?
- What benefits will come by slowing down and extending the deadline?
- What benefits will come from rushing to meet the deadline?

As you work through these thoughts, you may find that an adjustment is needed for your timeline. Pushing things back or rushing forward are both perfectly acceptable choices. Making the decision to adjust your target date sooner rather than later will help you to plan accordingly.

## Where am I in this process?

As discussed, some changes are thrown upon you with no choice but to gain your footing and then decide in which direction to head. Other changes are by your own design, and you can take your time.

Whichever change you are facing, it is critical to first know where you stand. Questions to consider are:

- Am I already behind the eight ball and playing catch up?
- Is there time to revisit earlier steps in the process?
- Which elements of this change are already in place?
- How far am I from the end goal of this change?

By understanding exactly where you stand, you can then strategize where to focus your time and energy. For example, if you are targeting a promotion in the office, but the job has already been posted, then the next steps need to be focused on applying and preparing for the interview process. However, if there is not yet an opening, you can take time to build your qualifications with education, certificates, and more experience. Where you are currently positioned related to the goal, determines your next steps.

## Why does this change need to happen?

This may be more obvious depending on the change you face. Some people may lose their job for one reason or another, but not by their choice. Same as for divorce that may force a need for change. Or an accident or illness. But really this question is more about making sure you understand your main motivations in life beyond the simple top-layer answers.

It is in answering this question, you sometimes find you do not care about this goal quite as much as you thought you did. Learning you do not have a strong *why* and abandoning your goal is a perfectly acceptable situation. But definitely a decision that is better made sooner than later.

If you doubt that, let me ask this: If you were to find out you were on the wrong course and needed to go back to the beginning, would you rather make that decision five miles down the road, or five hundred?

Considering why this change is important, go deep into your own personal why:

- Why is the outcome of this change important to me?
- Is the outcome of this change going to make me happy?
- Am I pursuing this change for myself or for others?
- If this change doesn't happen, what is the worst possible outcome?
- What is the best-case scenario if this change doesn't happen?

Again, having a shift in your thoughts as to whether this change really is important is perfectly acceptable. It is better to decide at the beginning of your journey that there are roads not worth exploring. You may find you are happier where you are, or learn that an entirely different change is needed.

### How will this change affect my life?

By now, you may have this answer. The previous questions have no doubt made you dig deeper into the idea of your new life after this change is complete. The purpose of this last question is to make you think through whether or not the way in which it will change your life is, in fact, the best outcome for you.

When you consider this question, look back through the previous questions and allow them to give you some guidance as to your answers:

- Who will this affect and is that what I really want?
- What will life look like with the best desired outcome?
- When this is done, will I be content?
- How much further down the process will I be on bigger goals?
- Will I feel like I am living true to my *why*?

Having these answers in front of mind will be the key to understanding how this change truly will affect your life. And as discussed earlier, if this exercise makes you rethink your goal, then that is better to revisit sooner than later.

Your goal is to make the best of your life changes, not to wade through any life change just to get to the other side of the river. When you tackle change in the right way, you will feel empowered and ready to take on the next and bigger challenges and goals in your life.

### Clearly Identify Change or Goal

So now that you have walked through each of the questions, take some time to fill out the worksheet.

Take your time, this is your life you are dealing with. I find it best to print up a copy or write in a journal while you reflect quietly on each question. Then once you have given thought to all of the aspects you need to consider, create a one or two sentence response to each of the questions on the form.

After you have worked through the entire form, set it aside for the night or maybe even a day or two while you reflect on the process. Then, when you come back to your answers, you may find you want to make some changes. Or perhaps, you will find resolution in your purpose and that you are pumped with new energy that makes you ready to jump into the next step.

Once you have this part done, the hard part actually, you get to start having some fun. No, I am not kidding. Doing this right, you should start to enjoy the process of making this change come to life.

The hardest part is deciding where you want to go and figuring out where you are in the process. Everything after that is simply gathering information, creating a plan, and sticking to it.

# MASTERING CHANGE: CLEARLY IDENTIFY

Clearly identify your goal. In order to be as clear and precise as possible, ask yourself the following questions:

**Change or Goal:** _____

Who does this change affect?

_____

_____

What is the best desired outcome from this change?

_____

_____

When do I need to be through with the changes I am facing?

_____

_____

Where am I in this process?

_____

_____

Why does this change need to happen?

_____

_____

How will this change affect my life?

_____

_____

Having worked through this worksheet, you may have more questions than answers. You may find your goal was not as clear as you first thought or that the change ahead is not so straight forward. This is okay. In fact, the more you question your reasoning, the more you can be sure you are taking the right course.

These questions brought to light sooner in the process are better addressed now than once you have spent hours of your time and possibly many dollars on your journey.

Make the changes necessary until you have a clear goal, a clear change in mind. Feeling confident in your goal is the first step towards a successful change.

*"Change the way you look at things and the things you look at change."*

~Wayne W. Dyer

# Honest Budget

Yes, it is time to look at your budget. This step is called looking at your *honest* budget because you need to get real with yourself about how you choose to budget your most valuable resources. In this program, *H* is for honest, not hopeful. This is not a time to plan out what you *hope* you have to work with.

Most often, the word budget is only used to refer to finances. Especially in terms of limited finances. But in this step, you will be looking at all of your most valuable resources: time, money, and energy.

Right about now, you may be thinking: *Wait, you said the hardest part was done.* I do stand behind my earlier statement of this being true. While working through budgets is not anyone's idea of fun, it is not especially hard once you know where you want to take yourself using those resources.

In this case, I challenge you to think of the word budget differently. Creating a budget is not meant to limit your spending or stifle your resources. In fact, it is quite the opposite. To create an honest budget is to make sure you are using them in the best way you can. Creating an honest budget allows you to make sure you have the time, money, and energy to do the things you really want. When done right, a budget provides choices and freedom.

Let's say you want to go see the newest movie this weekend. If you fail to set aside the time and save the money for the opening day, you will be disappointed when Saturday comes and you do not have the time nor the cash to go to the theater and catch that new blockbuster.

So, it is in budgeting your resources that you are ensuring you can get the most out of what you have to work with and live the life you want. Working through and understanding your honest budget is about creating choices, not limitations.

When you complete this step, you will know how much money you have to work towards your goal, how much time you have each week, and how much of your attention will be devoted to making it happen. You will be able to tell yourself: *I have fifty dollars per month and ten hours per week to make this dream happen, and it will be in my top three priorities to focus my energy on making it a reality.*

This step has three worksheets. Each is designed to give you an understanding of exactly what you have available. This will open choices as to how you will allocate those resources. The goal at the end of this exercise is to understand what you have to work with to tackle the life change ahead of you.

It is crucial that you be as realistic and honest about the figures you enter on the worksheets. For example, if the form asks how many hours you sleep, and you estimate six hours per night, when realistically you sleep nine hours, you will be shorting your time budget by three hours per day for a total of twenty-one fewer hours per week. This would be hours you expect to be able to apply to your goal. Later, when things are not working out, it will be because you did not fully account for one of your most precious resources: time. Again, be honest not hopeful.

Do the best you can. Be as honest as possible with yourself. But do not fret if your numbers are not exact. Remember this book is about change. And the one thing to remember is that you must be open to change. Even if it means coming back later and adjusting the plans you made to deal with changes.

With that in mind, let's get to working on your three budgets. First, you will walk through some things to consider for each element of your overall budget. Then, you can take the time to fill out the worksheet that correlates to each. Take as much time as you need. Like every step, work through the worksheet and then sit on your thoughts for a bit before you move on.

One method I find particularly effective with this step is to fill out the worksheets based on what you think your current situation is. Then track your activities for anywhere from a week to a month in order to see how well your ideal budget lines up with reality. At this point, you can adjust as needed. If you discover you spend more money on food than you planned, or the commute makes your workday an hour longer than you accounted for, change these lines.

## Financial Budget

Let's get the money talk out of the way. If you are like most people, the word budget is like hearing nails on a chalkboard. Who really wants to sit down and look at their budget? You would rather just keep your head in the sand and pray the bills get covered. But that is not reality.

There is good news. The reason you keep your head in the sand is out of fear of facing the truth about your numbers. Once you take a look at those numbers and know what you have available, you can move from operating in the dark to making clear, sound decisions based on the full understanding of what you have to work with.

When you understand your budget, you can leave the fear of being blindsided by financial surprises behind you. I have never felt I am a financial expert. In fact, this is exactly why looking closely at my budget is critical for me. It is those things which are harder for you to master, that you must monitor closely so they do not drag you down.

If you do not have the details for how you are spending your money, take time to gather this information. In order to complete the next worksheet, you will need a clear understanding of your monthly income as well as your expenses.

Depending on where you are with your finances, you may not have an immediate grasp of your situation. If you struggle to understand your cash flow and how to manage the basics of your income and bills, I recommend the book *Financial Joy* by Marcelle Allen. This interactive book is designed to take the pain out of understanding finances and dealing with money. Its workbook style is a hands-on approach to understanding and managing your money.

While completing the upcoming worksheet, you will encounter some spaces which are easy to fill in. These will be figures such as rent/mortgage and insurance which rarely change each month. Other numbers may be less clear as to what to account for. For example, your income might fluctuate each month depending on your schedule or potential for tips. Or how much you spend on food, gas, and extra activities.

When it comes to determining these numbers for myself, I believe it to be the safest course of action to err on the side of having less money to work with. In this way, anything extra you are able to come up with is a bonus. To achieve this, estimate lower than expected when it comes to income, and higher than you might need for expenses.

To give you an idea: if you earn anywhere between $1,600 and $2,000 dollars per month, use a figure of $1,600 based on the idea that you can at least count on this much. On the opposite side of the equation, estimate higher than average for the cost of expenses. If you typically spend $200 to $300 on gas, then you need to plan on the potential to have $300 per month available to spend.

When you follow this method, you are accounting for the potential worst-case scenario and allowing yourself a buffer zone in case you need it. You will feel much better having more money than you planned, rather than realizing you are short on funds and have to decide what you can pay and where to make cuts to get by until you come up with more money.

This step is called creating an honest budget for a reason. You must be completely honest and realistic with yourself when working through this worksheet. You will not be doing yourself any favors answering with the idealized numbers of where you hope to see your budget.

One area where I see this happen is when you look at how much money you spend on entertainment. Many times, you might not admit just how much goes into this budget. If you answer that you spend $100 per month on entertainment, accounting for a couple nights out to movies or dinner. Yet, you typically go out several nights per week, you will find your budget is obsolete before you even close this book.

It is also critical that you are honest about including all of the aspects of the costs of entertainment. When you take that night out on the town and account for a movie and dinner, did you also add in the cost of a rideshare, parking, and perhaps a babysitter? When you list what you do for entertainment, did you add in membership fees to streaming services for those shows you love to binge-watch? What about those magazines showing up in your mailbox?

I am not saying these all need to be cancelled. However, you must be realistic in what you are spending and for what reasons. In doing so, you can make choices to shift your money to support those things you want most in life. You can choose if you would rather read the latest celebrity gossip, or apply another ten dollars towards your next goal.

Creating an honest budget is about digging as deep as possible into any aspect of each line. While this sheet is simple, each space you fill out should add up to account for all of the money you are making and spending every month. It is crucial you step into facing your life changes knowing exactly what you have to work with. Not knowing this information is the base foundation for the fear that will erode your success.

With this in mind, take some time to complete the worksheet on the next page. When complete, subtract each expense from the income line. This gives you your bottom line: your remaining balance. This is the amount you will have to apply toward your life change.

# MASTERING CHANGE: HONEST BUDGET

It's time to create an honest budget for your money. Your balance is how much you have remaining to make this change happen. If you do not have enough remaining balance, see what numbers you can cut back on to free up money.

## Financial Budget:

| Item | Monthly Total |
|---|---|
| Income | _____ |
| Mortgage/Rent | - _____ |
| Auto | - _____ |
| Insurance | - _____ |
| Utilities | - _____ |
| Debt Payments | - _____ |
| Medical Bills | - _____ |
| Food | - _____ |
| Miscellaneous | - _____ |
| Entertainment | - _____ |
| Savings | - _____ |
| _____ (other) | - _____ |
| _____ (other) | - _____ |
| **Balance** | = _____ |

Dealing with finances first gets you through the hardest topic to face. If you are like many people who need to take some time to understand where your money is spent, then you may need to put this book down for a couple of days while you work through this step. I have been in this place myself so I totally understand.

The key to figuring out your budget is to find out what you have to work with when it comes to facing life changes and making goals happen. In the budget exercise, this answer comes in the last line: balance.

The ending balance is what you have remaining after accounting for everything you need as it relates to your money. This number is the money available to get through the change you face. If the remaining balance is $500, then this is what you will have to work with each month to enact the change ahead.

If you have $12, which is closer to the number I had when facing some of my most challenging changes, then you need to look at the reality of what you need to do.

At this point, you have a couple of options which may fluctuate with each scenario. First, let's look back at the budget and see if you can find more money. You can do this in two ways: increasing income or decreasing expenses. Basically, make more money, or spend less. This will take reviewing every line to see where you have the power to make changes to your flow of money. Can you pick up extra hours at work or get a second job? Can certain expenses be reduced or eliminated?

If in fact, you find that $12 is what you have to work with, then you will need to be very aware of how to make the most of $12. This is what I call the most valuable $12 ever.

If the number is smaller than you would like to see, which to be frank is the case most all of the time, then do not get discouraged. This will not always be the case. Looking at your budget is about learning what you have to work with in the first place. This will change and grow as you work through your change plan.

You may have to adjust your timeline or plans based on these numbers. Knowing this upfront and planning for it, puts you miles down the road. You are already way ahead of where you were before we started this exercise.

## Time Budget

Your time budget follows the same basic concept as the financial budget. It is all too easy to overlook the value of your time. It is the one resource you never get back. Time will continue to move forward at the same speed for all of us, whether you need to play catch up or not.

There is no pausing the clock on life. There is no holding the line while you get back up to speed. Time just continues marching forward at what may seem a cruel pace.

How is it that some people seem to have more time than others? Well, to be honest, they do not. They simply have learned how to better make use of their slice of pie.

Unlike the financial budget, your time budget will be factored on a weekly number. The good news is, everyone has the same starting number, 168 hours. That's right, everyone has the same number of hours to use every week. Now, what are you going to do with yours?

In order to best know how to use these hours, you must first know how you currently spend your time. Again, we can change and adjust as needed, as long as you are honest about whether or not this is a number you can commit to each week.

Just as before, there are some numbers that will be constant: how long you sleep, how many hours you work. While others you may have more control over, such as your time watching television or playing games.

As you work through the segments, be sure to account for all of your time. As with money, there can be additional factors to make sure you have accounted for. Let's say you work a forty-hour workweek, those forty hours are not all it takes to keep the job.

Having a job also requires getting prepped and out the door, as well as a commute every day. If you work forty hours on the job site, you may need to list an additional ten to twenty hours per week on the *Commute and Prep* line.

As before, be sure to account for spending more time on each activity than the minimum possibility. If your commute can range from one to two hours on any given day, plan on the two-hour number. Any commutes which are shorter will give you bonus time you can add to another activity. Even better, apply this time to focus on the change you are working towards.

The most common area I see people underestimate their time is for personal issues. These are things such as family time, errands, entertainment, self-care, and sleeping. Even though these can be the most important when it comes to your health and well-being, they tend to get prioritized last when planning your day.

Family time is important. Many of us naturally spend a great amount of time around our families, but do not set aside the time purposefully. This can include setting aside time to share your evening meal together, have a weekend activity, or support one another in each of your interests. Many times this crosses over into entertainment or even chores, but either way, plan for the time.

Self-care can range from setting aside much needed down-time to rest and recharge, to hitting the gym to keep that rock-hard body in shape. Keeping your body and mind fresh and healthy is a key component to your success. By budgeting your time to take care of yourself, including enough sleep, you are conditioning yourself to take on the journey ahead in your best state.

How many weeks have you been down to the bare minimum in your cupboard but just can't find time to get to the store? All too often, the things you need to keep functioning, such as clean laundry or fresh food, become stressful distractions from the time you can spare. These should not be surprises, yet they continually catch you having to squeeze them in at the last minute. In reality, this is simply a lack of setting aside the time to make them a priority. You push them to the bottom of the list favoring other things you need to spend time on or would rather do for entertainment.

As you work through the worksheet, consider the amount of time it will take to do each job well. If you know you realistically need two hours per week to grocery shop, set that time aside. If you need to rest and relax for three hours every night, write that down on your plan. Once you have an idea of where your time is going, you can begin making choices as to where you may want to adjust in order for your time to be spent in a way that is in line with your goals.

As with the financial budget, you will start with your total amount of time per week, 168 hours. Then subtract the amount of time spent on each line in order to arrive at your remaining balance. This balance will be the amount of time you will be able to dedicate to work through your life change.

Now that you have a head full of thoughts and questions, take a moment to work through the next page. Start with the amount of time you spend currently and make adjustments as you plan out where you would like to focus your time going forward.

# MASTERING CHANGE: HONEST BUDGET

It's time to create an honest budget for your time. Your balance is how much you have remaining to make this change happen. If you do not have enough remaining balance, see what numbers you can cut back on to free up more hours.

## Time Budget:

| Item | Weekly Total |
|---|---|
| **Total Hours** | **168** |
| Sleep Hours | -_____ |
| Work Hours | -_____ |
| Commute/Prep | -_____ |
| Family Time | -_____ |
| Shopping | -_____ |
| Cooking/Meal Prep | -_____ |
| Errands/Chores | -_____ |
| Miscellaneous | -_____ |
| Entertainment | -_____ |
| Self-Care | -_____ |
| _____ (other) | -_____ |
| _____ (other) | -_____ |
| **Balance** | =_____ |

Once you have worked through each aspect of the week, and where you spend your time, take a look at your balance. This will be how much time you have to navigate the changes ahead.

If you are left with four hours, yet you have a dream that requires you to spend twelve hours in school every week, then you need to find another eight hours. Perhaps you will have less time to rest and recharge or spend on entertainment and play. Maybe you will even have to sacrifice some of your family time.

The other option is to extend the amount of time it will take to reach your goal. If you cannot find the extra hours to go to school, you may find a six-month goal is now a two-year goal. It may not be the answer you want to hear, but accepting the circumstances to work within your budget is the first step to letting go of much of the pressure and stress that comes with working through life changes.

This is when taking a serious look at your priorities is needed. Below are a few questions to ask yourself when considering where to spend your time as you make these adjustments:

- Is this goal important enough to give up some of my family time?
- Do I need a set amount of time to rest and recharge in order to be working productively?
- If I spend less time with entertaining activities, will I become burned out?
- Can I find ways to combine activities such as commuting by train and resting or working on the ride?

Adjust as much and as often as necessary. Remember, this is a working budget. As you encounter changes to your needs, you can evolve your budget where possible. New demands may arise which require more of your time. You may find new priorities which you choose to dedicate time to. Or you may find a way to free up some hours which you can allocate to a new part of your budget.

Whatever the case is, whether you have two hours or ten hours per week, know that this will not be forever. If you are not so excited about the amount of time you have, you will be able to watch for opportunities to use your time as you wish. Unfortunately, I cannot give you more than 168 hours per week. That is just the reality of life and the facts of time. But with this budgeting tool, you may be able to find a few more hours to use as you like.

## Energy/Focus Budget

This part of the budget is more abstract than the numbers you have for your time and money worksheets. That said, this may be the most important piece of your budgeting exercise. For if you are not focusing your energy in the right places, nothing you want to come to pass will materialize. Your focus dictates how your time and money are spent. You could create a solid plan, but if your focus is spent elsewhere, you will find yourself losing precious dollars and hours every day.

The goal of this budget is to create awareness to where you focus your attention in an effort to make future choices spending energy on those things which you prioritize as most important. To find an understanding of where you currently focus energy, imagine you are sitting alone in an empty room. Picture a waiting room of sorts, where your only role is to wait your turn. While you wait, you are left undistracted with your thoughts.

Ask yourself these questions:

- Where will my mind drift to?
- What are the first things I am curious to check on?
- In this time, what do I feel compelled to think about most?
- What issues are hardest for me to stop thinking about?

The goal is to become familiar with your instincts as to what is getting the most attention in your mind. This is different than making a list of priorities. For example, the first priority may be your family or career, however, the reality is they may be the last thing that comes to mind when free time is available. It is not uncommon in this step for people to find they are giving more attention than they prefer to items which are low on their priority list.

This is not to say you do not value these things. We continually waltz on a tightrope when balancing our time between the things we value most and other less important demands. The trap comes when we fall off the rope by spending countless hours on insignificant things, while letting our priorities dangle.

Many times, the things you value most may not require immediate attention. You do not need to feel bad if your biggest life priorities are not what needs immediate attention. Think of those times when you have a large project to complete. You look past thoughts of family or health while you focus on the task at hand. This does not mean you toss your values to the side. It is just that you are needed more in one area right now than another.

However, when you allow less important things distract you, you step off the rope and fall far from your best self. Think about how easy it is to check on social media in the middle of the day, even when you have pressing work to do. It's not that you do not value work. It's simply that you are allowing less valuable causes to demand your focus and energy.

Once you have an understanding of where energy is drawn, you can channel attention towards those issues you most care about. You will identify those in the upcoming focus and energy worksheet.

The purpose of this exercise is to create a budget for how you would like to divide your focus in order to get this in line with your real priorities. Those things which are most important to you need to become the areas your mind comes to as soon as it has a free moment. In a way, you need to train your mind to bring focus and attention to those things you want most in life. First let's identify what those areas are for you.

To begin budgeting focus you need to identify those things you want to spend most of your energy on. The upcoming worksheet will help to identify and prioritize your focus. It is comprised of two sections.

In the ranking segment, simply rank the issues you prefer to spend your energy on. Rank these with one being the most important and ten being the item you prefer to give the least attention to. Change the names of the issues and topics as you see fit to suit your specific needs.

Once you have completed the top section, input your ranking into the triangle below. Simply list the item in the corresponding section of the triangle.

Take a few moments to complete the worksheet now:

# MASTERING CHANGE: HONEST BUDGET

In order to focus energy on those issues most needing attention, rank the categories below. Then complete the triangle.

## Energy/Focus Budget:

## Ranking:

| Work | Family | Relationships | Self-Care | Entertainment |
|------|--------|---------------|-----------|---------------|
| ___ | ___ | ___ | ___ | ___ |

| Goals | Finances | Social Media | Other | Other |
|-------|----------|--------------|-------|-------|
| ___ | ___ | ___ | ___ | ___ |

## Preferred Energy/Focus

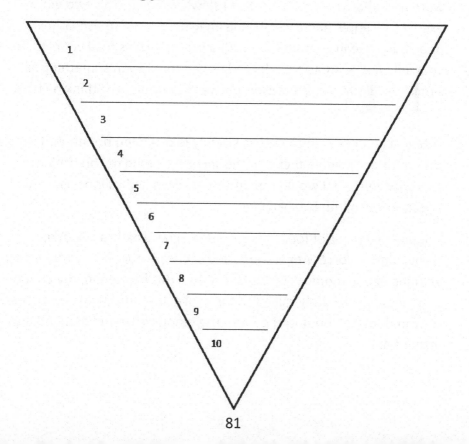

1 _____

2 _____

3 _____

4 _____

5 _____

6 _____

7 _____

8 _____

9 _____

10 _____

Visualize using the space in your brain like the inverted triangle from the previous worksheet. Those issues which you choose to focus on the most should take up the most space in your mind. Anytime you find yourself preoccupied with the bottom of the triangle, center your thinking back to one of the items in the top five.

In the aftermath of my divorce, I constantly found myself caught up in the negative. Walking through a store, I would get to the end of an aisle to be slapped in the face with a Father's Day display which reminded me I no longer lived with my kids. Or a song would play, bringing the anger and hurt of the relationship rushing in. It would take hold of my heart. As I felt my chest tighten with anger, I tried to think of anything else. The more I told myself to stop thinking about the hurt, the more it was in front of me. I found in these moments I needed to use a simple breathing exercise to bring my focus back to what I needed most.

*Heal yourself*, I would say as I concentrated on my breathing. One word as I inhaled. And the next as I slowly exhaled. This two word exercise is simple and can be done anywhere. I like to use either a verb or an adjective in combination with a noun. Such as heal yourself, love yourself, you're amazing, talented or beautiful. Even something as simple as *I'll survive*. Whatever you need to bring your thinking back to where you desire.

*Heal,* I would say to myself as I slowly take a deep breath in. Then as the air let out I would focus on the second word in my breathing exercise: *yourself.* I would repeat this as often and as long as needed to center my mind: *heal yourself.*

Being taken out of focus caught me off guard daily as I worked through my divorce. Anger, hurt, and sadness could take over without warning at any moment of the day. When this happened, my energy and focus immediately rallied to the cause. It seemed the more I tried to stop thinking about it, the more the emotions would demand my attention.

When it comes to focusing your attention, you cannot force yourself to stop thinking about anything in particular. You can, however, find ways to center your thinking in order to bring your mind back to being present on the matters at hand. Once you identify where you want your energy spent, you can apply some of the tricks below to get your thoughts in line with your goals.

Don't feel bad about how hard this step can be. Our fast-paced world, filled with alerts and notifications, is designed to pull your attention away from priorities to dilute your focus. Not to mention the emotional triggers you encounter daily. You need to come up with creative ways to train your brain to keep your priorities in front of mind.

Here are a few tips and tricks to consider:

- Use breathing exercises to center your thinking
- Replace distracting habits with new tasks
- Use printed materials to hang up as reminders
- Turn off alerts and notifications on your computer and phone
- Completely remove distracting apps from phone
- Schedule times to check email and messages
- Leave the phone off or in another room for blackout times
- Schedule a limited amount of time for social media

By understanding what pulls you away from the things you want to focus on, you can begin to eliminate those distractions. While it may seem remedial to remove apps or set alarms to keep yourself on track, you just may need this discipline in place long enough to break distracting habits.

While your brain has limited capacity for attention, you need to push the important things to the top, where most of the mind space is used. Looking back at your inverted pyramid, whenever you find yourself being sidetracked by items in the bottom five, use exercises to re-center your thinking. By doing so, you are taking control of your thinking. You are empowering your mind to choose where you want to focus your thoughts.

Your focus budget overrides the outcome of your time and financial budgets. In essence, they all go hand in hand. If you plan to spend four hours working on your goal this week, yet you allow your focus to be eaten up with social media or entertainment, you will find those four hours are lost to you forever. Controlling how you focus your energy will dictate the level of success you have with not only your budgets, but also, your goals.

## Completed Budgets

Now that you have worked through each of the honest budget portions of the Mastering Life Changes System, you have an idea of exactly what you are working with. You can look at your worksheets and easily explain how much money you have per month and just how many hours you have per week to work on making this change happen. You also know on which issues you prefer to focus your energy.

If you do not feel you have enough in any one area, take a look at your budget and see where there is room to adjust your spending or time commitments to give yourself more resources to work with.

Budgets are working plans. You can come back to this step at any point as your situation changes. I recommend checking back every week as you get started and then once a month after that.

Ask yourself a few questions as you review your budgets:

- Is this budget still relevant to my current situation?
- Was I realistic in my distribution of money, time, and energy?
- Which lines do I need to adjust to account for more time or money?
- Which areas did I account for more than I needed to?
- How does this affect my bottom line?
- Do I need to adjust my plan going forward based on these updated numbers?
- How have my energy and focus priorities changed?

Refer back to this as often as needed. Many times you might start to feel a crunch week after week before realizing the issue is needing to rework your budget. This could materialize as funds dry up faster than expected, or by continually running out of time to finish everything on your list. Building the framework is just the beginning. As life continues to change and your plan evolves, you need to adjust your resources accordingly.

*"Change is the law of life. And those who only look to the past or present are certain to miss the future."*

~John F. Kennedy

# Assets & Resources

Whether or not you have as much time and money at your disposal as you prefer, I hope you feel empowered in knowing exactly what you have to work with as you begin the next step.

That next step is to gain a thorough understanding of what resources you will require in order to make this change a reality. You do this by first assessing the needs of your upcoming change. Then you take stock of everything you have access to. This will allow you to create your arsenal.

## Assets & Resources Needs Assessment

When looking at your assets and resources, you first take a good, hard look at what is needed to get through the changes ahead. You do this by completing the *Assets & Resources Needs Assessment* on page 87. In this exercise, you will gain a clear picture of what you require to make your goal a reality. Stay focused on what is needed without getting caught up in whether or not you have the tools currently available. You will work through that part in the rest of the exercise.

It is also important to understand every situation is complex and unique. Your change is defined by where you want to end up as it relates to where you currently are. The recipe for your change strays from the norm even further when you add in the variables of any combination of ingredients you have on hand as opposed to what you will need to source.

With each goal unique, it follows that your needs will be completely different. Some changes may require heavy financing for education, investment, and expenses. While other changes require outside resources from the community or demand more time. Depending on your goal, you may need several physical assets or very few. You will find that you may be running out of space to write in one area, while you have more than enough in another. Keep this in mind as you work through each section of the assessment.

Pull out a paper and pen to do some brainstorming and crunching numbers before filling out this page. The worksheet is a simplified form to compile an overview of your needs. For example, you may need to hire a service, buy equipment, or pay for education. I recommend brainstorming your list on a blank page, then sorting out which category each of these needs best fits into.

With that in mind, let's get started with the assessment.

### Skills Needed

You will need skills to take you to your goal. Some of these skills may be more obvious. If you are moving, can you physically lift boxes? If you are opening a business, do you understand accounting or marketing? If you are expecting a child, do you have parenting skills?

Again, this is not the place to focus on what you do not have. Simply take time to brainstorm about everything you might need in order to make your change as successful as you can possibly imagine.

One way to work through finding the skills you need is to walk through the process of the upcoming change by writing it out as a story. Use detail to explain what you expect to encounter step by step, how you will implement the change ahead, and what tools and skills you will use. Once you have written out your story, read it through and make notes along the side, noting each time a skill was used. Then add these skills to the list of needed skills.

If you are not much of a writer or fear you do not have any idea of what will come, do this same exercise by watching a video such as a documentary or a biography highlighting a person who went through a similar change. Keep your notepad handy and make notes along the way.

Use emotion to your benefit. If you find yourself feeling fear or anxiety about any part of the process, make a note and ask yourself why. Is there a skill needed you fear you do not have? Be sure to get it added to the list so when you are ready to seek out the resources needed it will not be missed. Now make sure all of your notes are added to the list of the skills needed.

I cannot stress enough that it is your job to not get overwhelmed at this time. This part of the process is much like cleaning out a closet that needs to be organized. You must first make a big mess and face the ugly truth before you can put everything in its proper place. You have to know what you are dealing with before you can create a plan of attack.

### Physical Assets Needed

You may need physical assets to make this change a reality. If you are writing a book you need a computer, or at least a pen and paper. If you are moving across the country, you need a truck. Perhaps you are opening a store and need to rent a space, buy fixtures, and inventory. Whatever you are working through, you need some form of assets.

As you work through this step, look back at the story you wrote or the film you watched. Note where items were needed along the way. Be sure to include everything you need, even if you already have it in your possession. Keeping one master list will help you understand the scope of what you are undertaking. This will also prove to be empowering when you find you already have items you can cross off the list.

Be sure to include everything you will require to get the job done. This does not mean every item will need to be purchased. For example, you do not need to buy a moving truck in order to relocate. Renting or borrowing is perfectly acceptable and typically a more feasible option. However, you need to keep everything you need in mind so as you gather supplies for each step of the way, you do not overlook a critical tool.

*Projected Financial Costs*

Changes and goals come with costs. Not all are obvious and not all changes have big budgets. Some changes will have very little financial impact, but that does not mean you should not consider any potential costs that could be involved.

A change such as a promotion may not seem as though it comes with financial costs. Before reading this book, you might only see the financial change from a promotion as a raise in pay. But what costs might you encounter? Could you need to spend money on a more professional wardrobe? Might you need to invest some time and money in furthering your education or training courses?

In the case of a relationship change, some costs might be staring you in the face. Will you need to move out on your own and pay higher rent? Will you have to pay an attorney to file for divorce? While these expenses are large, there are also smaller things to think through. Even if you had a simple breakup which does not require so many costs. For example, will you be going out with friends more and need to budget for that? Perhaps you need to plan a weekend getaway to reset your mind?

As you see, not all costs are large or obvious, but taking time to think through potential spending needs will allow you to plan. Once you have a clear idea of what your goal will cost, you can successfully plan to navigate your way to the best desired outcome.

As you work through this section, remember your expected cost should account for all of the aspects related to this change. Will you need to buy a different car, relocate, or spend money on training?

Each of these costs factor into the total cost of the change. Understanding this upfront will help as you layer in the numbers from your financial budget. The total cost spread over your timeline will help you know if you have enough funds to make this goal a reality.

This can be where you start to get discouraged or feel a bit overwhelmed. I urge you to not let those feelings hold you back. When you get a reality check, you often find your dreams are not as close as you hoped. However, working your way through the rest of this step, you will find empowerment in the assets and resources at hand: resources you bring to the table, and those you have access to with the help of your community and support network.

The real test here is to create a clear list of what you need for your success without getting caught up in what you do not have. You will work on creative ways to find those resources as you complete the rest of this step over the next few exercises.

*Time Investment Required*

How much time will your goal require? To answer this correctly, think about how much time will be used in the process, not how long will it take. If you answer in a total length of time you hope to target, such as six months, then you are not doing this section correctly.

When answering for time, you need to understand time as a resource you have to work with each week. If you intend to complete school in two years, you have to understand the level of time you will be spending per week in order to make this happen.

For example, can you complete your courses by spending ten hours per week for two years? If your answer is yes, then you can have a realistic goal to finish school in two years, if you can dedicate the ten hours per week. If not, then you need to find more time in your week or extend your deadline.

This is the first step in viewing your time as a precious resource. You choose how to spend it on each of your priorities. List out each aspect of different elements of your goal. Then assign an expected amount of time invested on each of these elements. This will help you discover the required amount of time needed per week or month.

I have had to do this very thing when facing each aspect of my business. Podcasting, networking, marketing, and writing, all have specific demands of my time. It is easy for any one of these to dictate a bigger segment of time on a given week. By assessing how much time I expect to spend on each, I can be realistic as to whether the investment of time is worth including in my long-term plans.

With these thoughts in mind, grab a notebook and start working your way through creating the list of everything you will need to make your goal a reality. Then recap your findings on the worksheet on the next page:

# MASTERING CHANGE: ASSETS & RESOURCES

You will require many resources in order to own the change you are facing. Some will be obvious from the beginning, while others will present themselves over the course of your process. Create a list of everything you foresee which may be needed to achieve your goals.

## Assets & Resources Needs Assessment:

Skills Needed:

_____

_____

_____

Physical Assets Needed:

_____

_____

_____

Projected Financial Costs:

_____

_____

_____

Time Investment Required:

_____

_____

_____

## Assets & Resources Worksheets

It is now time to pull together everything at your fingertips to manage change and make your goals happen. Whether you have ten dollars or a hundred dollars to work with, you have even greater value available to you through your skills, your assets, and your community.

This step can be eye-opening as it relates to what you bring to the table. This is not the time to get caught up on what you do not have. Simply take stock of what you either have or have access to. This is how you determine exactly what you can work with when you get into the following steps to create your map and work your way past roadblocks. Focusing on the things missing only creates discouragement which ultimately leads to limiting beliefs.

This exercise is broken into two different segments: internal and external resources. In order to complete this section, you will need two different-colored pens or highlighters. You will use these separate colors in the upcoming steps to organize where you will allocate each of the assets and resources from your needs assessment.

## Internal Assets & Resources

First, look at internal resources. These are the assets you own and the skills you possess. Some of these answers are probably already on your mind from working through the previous exercise. In reflecting on what you require, it is natural to marry your needs to your ability to fulfill those needs. By taking a deep dive into what you bring to the table for yourself, you will find a sense of empowerment.

The first line is as easy as looking back to your budget worksheets to find what you have available in each of these three resources. You have already worked through your budget for finances, time, and focus. Your balance and ranking from these budgets are transferred here as resources for you to work with.

Review your finance and time worksheets to find your remaining balance for each. This becomes your resource in this step. If you have two hours per week and twenty dollars per month to work with, enter those numbers here.

Then, look to your *Energy and Focus Budget* to find your ranking for the change you are facing. This ranking shows how you have prioritized how much of your energy and attention this change will warrant in your life. Enter your ranking number from the energy budget worksheet here.

Next, take stock of the other assets and resources you can provide for yourself. As a starting point, refer back to your *Assets and Resources Assessment*. As you review each section of your assessment, ask yourself if this is something you already possess. If the answer is yes, then add it to the appropriate line of your Internal Assets worksheet. Highlight or underline each item with a colored pen on the assessment page as you identify you have it in your arsenal.

For example, if your life change requires you to be proficient with computer skills, and this is a skill you have developed, then highlight it on your assessment and add this under personal skills on the resource worksheet. Work your way through each section of the needs assessment to cover anything you have anticipated being required. Account for anything you can provide yourself, highlighting each item as you go.

Once you have looked through all of the anticipated needs, review the assets and resources you possess, but did not include as being needed for this goal. For example, do you own a home or car which could be tapped into through a sale or loan if you determine the funds are better served elsewhere. Or perhaps you are skilled in the area of sales, but did not foresee needing to use this skill for this change. If it is a skill you possess, it might be useful in order to get the help you need. In this way, you begin to turn your current skills and assets into resources for the purpose of realizing your goals.

I cannot stress enough that this is not a time to focus on what you do not bring to the table, simply ask yourself: What do I have to work with?

Take some time to work through the Internal Assets and Resources worksheet on the following page:

# MASTERING CHANGE: ASSETS & RESOURCES

You have more resources than you may even realize. Internal resources are things you own or bring to the table. Create a list of everything you possess that may be of help to achieve your goals and navigate change.

## Internal Assets & Resources:

**Item**

Time: _____ per _____      Finances: _____ per _____      Focus Rank: _____

Personal Skills:

_____

_____

Physical Assets:

_____

_____

Personal Financial Assets:

_____

_____

Other Assets/Resources:

_____

_____

## External Assets & Resources

Knowing what you bring to the game is only the first step. Next, you get to take a look at all the help available to you. This is what is referred to as your external assets and resources. By considering your external resources you identify what you can pull together from your network, your community, or even public services in order to gather anything and everything you need to make this change happen.

A great way to begin this process is to look back to your *Assets and Resources Assessment*. Everything left without a highlight or underline represents the resources you need to get creative in sourcing.

Look at each item from the assessment and then decide which category you can use to fill your needs on the *External Resources Worksheet* on page 96. Some of the items that need sourcing may fit into more than one category. This is great! Add them to as many places as possible. This gives you a chance to have more than one way to get what you need.

Once you find a potential source for each item from the initial assessment, again highlight it or underline it. But this time use a different color. This will allow you to look back at your assessment and easily see which items you will bring to the table and which items you need to source elsewhere.

### Online Resources

In today's world of being connected, you have access to more than ever before. Believe it or not, you can use social media for more than just watching crazy cat videos.

When you look at online resources you need to be specific in how you can use each aspect of your virtual world. Be as specific as possible when reflecting on these questions:

- What skill do I not possess in which I can watch online tutorials or take classes online in order to teach myself?
- Is there a social media group I can join in order to develop support or ask the questions I need?

- What research can be done through a search engine?
- Which company or institutions' sites should I visit?
- Who has successfully made this journey that I can follow online?
- How can I use social media to get the word out that I need help?

With all of the online resources available, you may need additional space in your journal or with a separate piece of paper.

*Community Resources*

It is common in today's society to think you have to do everything online. In a world of technology, it can be easy to lose sight of the value your local community offers. In this section, list anything you can access in order to build your arsenal. This is after all what you are doing: arming yourself for the battles ahead.

Your community is bigger than you realize. When working through this question, start with those in your inner circle and then work your way out. For example, reflect on what friends and family could offer before looking to acquaintances and strangers.

As you look back on what you need to achieve your goals and undoubtedly find missing items, ask yourself: Whose door can I knock on to find help?

Here are some questions to consider:

- What services or resources can my friends and family provide?
- Which businesses might have services or resources available?
- Can I find a class or support at a local community center?
- What services are available through local schools or libraries?
- Which networking groups or support groups might be beneficial to join?
- How can I spread the word of my needs through my local network?

Whether using a formal service such as free computer access at the library or the knowledge of a local networking group or casually using the help and advice from friends, your community resources are the most powerful available. Often times these services and support are free or can be paid by simply being involved and returning a favor. The value of your support network through times of change is immeasurable.

### Outside Financial Resources

Your dream might be bigger than you have the funds to pay for. Maybe you are years away from having enough funds, or perhaps you are just a few dollars short. Either way, you may need to seek external financial help.

While a loan may be the first thing that comes to mind, there are other ways to come up with the money. As you think through your specific life change, consider these questions:

- Are grants available to support my mission?
- If I need schooling, are scholarships available?
- Do I need to take a loan out to support my goal?
- Which services can I offer to raise funds?
- Who might be willing to invest in my goal?
- Can I generate funds by sharing my journey through a blog or podcast?
- Which local businesses may be willing to sponsor me?
- How can I pick up more hours or get a second income?

Often times, finances are an overwhelming topic which you would much rather avoid facing altogether. However, by digging deep into the possibilities of pulling funds together, you will find there is more than one way to fund your journey.

### Other Assets & Resources

As you have worked through the *big three,* if you will, when it comes to finding external support for your change, take a moment to consider your friends, family, and community. Are there available resources you know of, but did not list in one of the previous questions? Load those here whether you see an immediate need for them or not.

Reflect on these questions to help:

- Which of my friends are connected well in the community?
- Who are the most creative and resourceful people I know?
- Who has tools or supplies which I may be able to use?
- When are local events happening which I could attend to grow my support network?
- Which organizations in my community have I not explored?

As you move along and face the change ahead, you do not always know what challenges you will face. With these challenges will come a need for additional resources. Being aware of this will help you be prepared to find solutions when you need them.

Now take a moment to fill in your answers on the following page:

# MASTERING CHANGE: ASSETS & RESOURCES

You have more resources than you may even realize. External resources are available to you through other sources. Create a list of everything you have access to through your community and support network that may be of help to achieve your goals and navigate change.

## External Assets & Resources:

Online Resources:

_____

_____

_____

Community Resources:

_____

_____

_____

Outside Financial Resources:

_____

_____

_____

Other Assets/Resources:

_____

_____

_____

Looking back at the worksheets you have just completed, you will see you have three distinctive lists. First, you have your needs clearly identified. Followed up with a listing of what you already have, and then a list of where to source the remaining needs.

Revisiting your Assets & Resources Needs Assessment, you may have items left that you have not yet found a source for. These will be the items which have not yet been highlighted or underlined. Before you can move on, you need to create a plan for how to address these needs.

You will have to find these externally as you do not possess them currently. First you must prioritize these. Ask yourself these questions for each remaining item.

- Is this item critical to my success?
- Will this item be needed before I can start on my goal?
- At what point in the process is this item needed?
- Will I be able to obtain it along the way?

By understanding how critical, and when the item is needed, you can sort out what the next step should be. If your life change is to enhance your education, and it requires $10,000 for tuition, then your change plan will need to start with coming up with these funds. However, if you have $5,000 you may be able to get started while you work on raising the remaining funds.

If they are not mission critical, you can get started while still needing to find resources. Or if they will not be mission critical until a certain point, you can get a plan in place to source them by the time they are needed. The key is to be realistic in seeing what will be needed and having a plan in place to acquire it.

The problem enters when you get started thinking things will materialize as needed without planning on how to make it happen. Even worse, is starting down a path towards a goal while not having considered any of the tools you need. This method leaves you frustrated from day one, feeling like the world is working against you, when in reality you did not prepare for the journey ahead.

Once you have completed this portion, you are well on your way to mastering your life changes. You have a better understanding of your relationship with change. You know what you can commit to your goal from your time, finances, and your energy. And now you even have a clear idea of what you have to work with and where to find the remaining resources you need. In the next chapter, you will use this foundation to chart the strategy to tackle the changes ahead.

*"The people who are crazy enough to think they can change the world are the ones who do."*

~Steve Jobs

# Navigation Map

Let's step back to recall the three ways in which change can happen: a tide slowly creeping in, a tsunami, or a ship preparing to set sail. Whether your change crept in like a tide or swept over you like a tsunami, you have brought yourself back to shore by working through the previous steps. You have taken control of the course of your life and prepared yourself to embark on the next leg of the voyage.

Regardless of how this change began, you are now in the optimum position to take control. You are now standing at the shore with your ship packed, ready to set sail with compass in hand. All that is left to do is to chart the course for the changes in your life, and embark on your journey.

This is where you take action. You may be thinking, it's about time. But without all of the proper planning which you worked through in the previous chapters, your plans would be destined to fail. Since you have read this far, you have put in the work needed to make your plan successful.

So what is the next step? That is entirely up to you. This answer depends on where you are going, when you need to get there, and where you are now.

## Charting Your Course

When it comes to charting your course, you cannot simply state where you want to end up and when you expect to arrive. Imagine you are relying on your GPS to lead you from Seattle to New York. It wouldn't start you on the road with the first direction stating, "Arrive in New York in 2,857 miles." If this was how your GPS system worked, you would be lost all of the time.

However, this is exactly how most of us treat our goals. We tend to state the time we plan to arrive with no plan as to the first steps in the journey. A reliable navigation system first meets you where you are, then guides you step by step through each turn you need to make along the way. This is exactly what you need to do for yourself.

Meet yourself where you are. Don't jump in miles down the road, expecting to get caught up in time to follow directions the rest of the way. Start at the place you currently occupy and identify the very first move you need to make.

Creating your map requires sorting out all of the steps needed to get to your goal while identifying points to evaluate and evolve as you go. You will break this process down by working through the following three worksheets: *Mapping Considerations, Navigation Chart,* and *Action Steps*.

## Mapping Considerations

Before mapping out the course towards your goal, you have to revisit a lesson discussed previously regarding acceptance. While you might have come to terms with accepting the change you are facing, you still need to accept what is and is not within your control to move your plan forward.

When it comes to charting your course, there will be certain variables outside of your control which you must not only accept, but learn to work with. There will also be obstacles in your way which you must plan to navigate past.

*Things Outside of Your Control*

Imagine you are the captain of a ship which is about to set sail through the Caribbean. When planning your course, you need to understand which things are out of your control in order to account for a safe and successful voyage. For example: the weather, the direction the wind is blowing, and the force of the wind. With the change you are facing in life now, these represent things outside of your control.

When starting my own business, I spent months being held up on this step. I would create a goal, implement a plan of action, and then lament about why my results were less than stellar. Looking back, I can see with clarity that I had not accounted for, nor accepted those things which were outside of my control.

Some things will be more obvious when you consider where your limits of control are: the passing of time, your access to financial resources, or the scope of your skills in the areas needed. Yet, the bigger setbacks for me came through the more subtle delays. In particular were the delays from getting help from others.

I had a timeline I needed to hit for my goals to become a reality. When I reached a point where I needed help, I would call in a friend or hire a professional. Then I would find my forward momentum halted as they had their own projects to work on before getting to mine. This caused frustration on my part as I watched my dream sit on hold while someone else worked it into their priority list.

However, I learned two important lessons in this time. First, as well-meaning as others are, my goal will never be as important to them as it is to me. And second, in planning my action steps, I need to account for the timelines of others. This holds true, whether you are requesting help from a friend just as much as if you are buying a product or service from a business. Everyone has a timeline they are working on and their timeline may not fit easily into yours.

By acknowledging anything outside of your control, you can accept the boundaries within which you must work. Even better, you can find ways to work around them in order to expand those limits. Accept what you cannot control. Not so that you can limit your success, but rather so your success is not limited by those boundaries.

*Things You Can Control*

You may feel at the mercy of the world when looking at all of the things outside of your control. However, as you captain your ship, there are many variables you can control. These might be decisions such as when to depart, who you hire for the crew on your voyage, or when to pull into a safe harbor to rest and recharge.

There is power in making decisions. Though we often feel powerless to make the choice we prefer. By first accepting what is outside of your control, you open the power to make the best decisions for your journey within the realm of what you can control.

When looking at this section, be sure to stay aware of your own expectations. Controlling these is critical to not setting yourself up for disappointment. For example, if you plan to sail from Florida to California and expect to arrive after only a day of sailing, you are planning to be disappointed. Controlling your expectations by accepting that it will take much longer, will remove the emotion of disappointment which undermines your confidence in your abilities. Though it may not seem to be the case, you do have the power to control your own expectations.

*Events and Dates*

Many of the things outside of your control are those boulders in life which we have no choice but to work around. If you plan to go to school, you are at the mercy of the school schedule. If your goal is to speak at a national conference, you are bound by the timeline of when that event is being held. These are nonnegotiable elements of your plan.

Just like a ship's captain who will need to look at masses of land to avoid in order to not run the ship aground, you will need to look ahead at these obstacles as you chart your course. Understanding and accepting elements of your journey which you have no choice but to navigate past will set you up to plan a successful voyage.

Considering the change you now face, reflect on which things are set in stone. Which elements will you need to incorporate into your plan? Are there events you are required to attend? Do you need to be in a certain place by a certain date? These are just a few of the questions to ask yourself as you work through the first worksheet to create your *Navigation Map*.

Now, fill out the *Mapping Considerations* worksheet on the next page:

# MASTERING CHANGE: NAVIGATION MAP

Complete the form below by listing the elements of this change you can control, those you cannot, as well as the events or dates to consider which you will need to work around.

## Mapping Considerations:

Change/Goal: _____ Completion Date: _____

**Outside of Control** _____

_____

_____

_____

_____

**Within My Control** _____

_____

_____

_____

_____

**Events and Dates** _____

_____

_____

_____

_____

Having a clear idea of what you can and cannot control sets the perimeters of your plan. This gives you the structure you need to work within while allowing you visibility to the moves you can make to realize your vision. In a way, this sets the rules of the game. With these in mind, you can now build the structure for your map.

## Navigation Chart

Imagine if you will, that you are about to embark on a journey and you have entered the destination into your GPS. As it starts to show you directions one step at a time, you decide to switch to the course overview and see the satellite view of the entire trip. This is what you will do in this step: zoom out from the step-by-step to see the overall plan.

The first step in creating your navigation map is to lay out the plan in general terms. You have previously defined your goal in the *Clearly Identify Change or Goal* exercise on page 56. In this same exercise you determined when you need to have your goal completed. Start filling out the *Navigation Chart* on page 108 by entering this information.

You will enter your goal as well as the target completion date both at the top and bottom of this worksheet. This will identify where you need to be by a certain time-frame. You can choose a date such as the day and year, or choose a time period such as twelve months from start.

I find it useful to use a time period rather than a date initially when working out the plan for goals which I have not yet started to put in place. Then, once I am ready to move forward with the project, I convert the timeline to dates in order to be more aware of time constraints and other obstacles.

By following this strategy, you can layout the timeframe of a project and then look for conflicts in your calendar before setting your plan in motion. For example: I plan to set sail in nine months, however that would land me in the middle of hurricane season. With a plan that will take nine months to implement, I can adjust my start date in order to be complete and ready to set sail at the optimum time.

As your plan is now, you have an extremely thin shell. You know where you are, and where you want to be. The next thing to do is build a frame to support your shell. Before you can decide what steps will need to be taken to get from point A to point B, you will need to account for those events and landmarks which you will need to plan around. This could be hurricane season, or if you are going to school, the day registration is required.

Refer to your *Mapping Considerations Worksheet* (page 104) to guide you through which events, dates, and obstacles need to be considered. Add these into the upcoming *Navigation Map* in the *Landmarks and Steps* column by identifying approximately where they will fall in your process. Once these are entered, you can work around them with the appropriate action steps to walk you towards your goal.

In this exercise it is important to stay focused on the big picture. Do not try to imagine every possible obstacle or outcome you could ever encounter. We will tackle those in the next segment. This is time to look at the big picture, the satellite view.

After dropping in the boulders, as I like to call them, you can list the basic action steps you will need to take in order to complete your goal. Work backwards from the bottom of the list towards the top. Starting with the goal, ask yourself: What will I need to have complete before this is a reality? Then identify that step in the process. Continue to work your way backwards, each time asking what needs to be done before this step comes to fruition. Continue this until you get to the top of the page and ultimately meet yourself where you are now.

While working your way through the process, look at each landmark or event you have already listed and determine if the action you are considering needs to be complete before or after you have passed that boulder.

If your goal is to open a restaurant, you may have entered a completion timeframe of one year from now. Your end goal is opening day. You would enter landmarks such as when you need to have permits, or how soon you need to have staff hired in order to train them. Perhaps your restaurant supports a seasonal crowd, so you need to be open by a certain date or you miss the business for that year.

Each of these would have been boulders to work past. Considering these, you would then enter when to start each phase of the process. You need to apply for permits before you can start construction. Employees need to be hired before they can be trained. They cannot be trained until your menu is decided and product is on hand for production. But you cannot bring product in until you have passed the required inspections.

There is a flow that must be followed. Each step builds on the previous progress. The following action cannot take place without the proper foundation being built. Creating your *Navigation Map* is your way of seeing the foundation and planning in a way that continues to grow your dream on the work you have previously put into it.

With this in mind, refer back to your *Mapping Considerations* and fill out the worksheet on the next page:

# MASTERING CHANGE: NAVIGATION MAP

Create an overview of your plan below. List your target end date at the bottom and work your way back from there in increments of weeks or months. You will pause to evaluate every three steps.

## Navigation Chart:

Change/Goal: _____ Completion Date: _____

**Time Period:**                    **Landmarks and Steps:**

_____          _____

_____          _____

_____          _____

_____          _____

_____          _____

_____          _____

_____          _____

_____          _____

_____          _____

_____          _____

_____          _____

_____          _____

**Target Date**                    **Change/Goal Achieved**

_____          _____

## Action Steps

Having charted your course, you can now break down each leg of your journey into smaller actionable steps. This is where the rubber meets the road, if you will.

The following worksheet will guide you through creating your *Action Steps*. Each step of the way asks you to plan through four simple elements: identify the step, assign a timeline, plan the use of resources, and prepare for issues. You will work through this process repeatedly as you work past each landmark you identified on your *Navigation Chart* in the previous exercise.

### Identify Step

Keeping in mind where you are starting from and where you want to go, you need to identify what the first action to take will be. As you review your *Navigation Chart*, concentrate on the first time period.

If you are opening a restaurant, the first thing you may need to do is learn to cook. Perhaps you do not have the funds to pay for culinary school. Then your first step will be to raise funds through a second job or by applying for scholarships. If you are past this phase of the process, then look to see what your next immediate need is in order to make this dream a reality.

The page provided allows for four steps. You may need to set a course beyond four, or break down these steps into sub-steps. Use your journal or make extra copies as needed in order to capture the entire picture. However, do not get caught up in the detail work beyond four main steps at a time. More than this becomes overwhelming and can easily lead to paralysis through analysis.

Keeping your attention on the next four steps allows you to see three steps ahead while focusing on the task at hand.

In the example to open a restaurant, your first four steps might be as follows:

- Step 1- Raise funds for culinary school
- Step 2- Research schools
- Step 3- Apply to schools
- Step 4- Begin schooling

Obviously, there will be much more to deal with when it comes to opening a restaurant. But until you have dealt with the immediate needs, the steps that follow become a distraction. You cannot allow for distractions to pull your focus away from making your goal come true, especially when the distraction is the goal itself.

*Assign Timeline*

With a clear idea of the first steps you need to take in your journey, you now need to assign times to when you expect to have each step complete. Take a look through each of the steps you identified and consider the most reasonable time it should take to complete each task.

Remember time is one of your resources. When planning for the use of resources it is best to overestimate your need. If you think a task should be completed in two weeks, plan for an extra week to allow yourself time to recover from any setbacks along the way.

By building in extra time for each step to be complete you help to manage your expectations. This is critical in saving you from unneeded disappointment and stress in the future. Typically your biggest let-downs are due to your own unreasonable expectations.

Coming back to the example to open a restaurant, the timelines for the first four steps might look like this:

| Action Step | Timeline |
|---|---|
| 1: Raise funds for school | 6 Months |
| 2: Research schools | 2 Months |
| 3: Apply to schools | 2 Months |
| 4: Begin schooling | 8 Months |

Some actions may be able to be completed simultaneously, as is the case with steps one and two above. This is great when you have many things that need to be completed before you can move on to the next step. But you must be sure to account for the time you have per week to do so. If you are able to work through two steps at once, make sure you have enough hours available and enough available energy to focus on both before committing to doing so.

*Resources Needed*

Before you step into any action, you need to have a clear understanding of the resources you will need. If there is a resource you need in order to proceed which you do not have, then getting that resource must be covered in an earlier step.

For example, if you plan to enroll in school but do not have the tuition money, then the first step needs to be raising the funds needed. Only then are you equipped and ready to move forward.

As you work through creating a list of resources for each step, picture yourself walking through every aspect of completing the step. As you do so, note anything you will use to complete the process. In the current example, the resources needed for step two should look something like this:

- Step 2- Research Schools: Resources Needed
  - Computer
  - Phone
  - Transportation
  - Time
  - Money
  - People to interview

Refer back to both your *Internal and External Assets and Resources Worksheets* on pages 91 and 96. These will sort out where to find the support you need. Having done this work previously, you have already identified where to source the necessary help. If you discover additional needs, add them to the lists where appropriate.

In this example, you would need a computer to look up information about potential schools online. You would need to use a phone to call and make inquiries. In order to visit the campus, you would need access to transportation which will require time and money. You would also want to speak with people who have attended the school or work in the industry in order to get a better understanding of what the school can provide.

Each of these is a resource you need in order to complete this step. You have many of these at your disposal without giving it much thought, like your phone for instance. But understanding what you have at hand is a powerful thing in a time when you can easily be overwhelmed.

### Prepare for Issues

No one likes to think about how things can go wrong. However, not looking down the road to see the potential for setbacks is one of the easiest ways to be caught off guard when they occur. The next chapter will deal with how to get past them. In this step, you need to create an awareness that they will most likely happen.

Not every step will be laden with hurdles and roadblocks. Some will definitely have more than others. But planning for them as best you can allows you to see them as part of the process rather than an omen of doom.

When looking ahead at each step, consider what may become an obstacle. When you are facing a change that is new to you, I find the absolute best way to know what these could be is to talk to people who have been down the road before. Ask questions such as what roadblocks did they encounter and what unexpected events occurred.

Looking at step two of the example, some anticipated issues could be as follows:

- Step 2- Research Schools: Anticipated Issues
    - Connection problems on the internet
    - Trouble finding reliable information
    - No one available to answer questions
    - Scheduling conflicts do not allow to tour the campus

It is in having an understanding of what might hold you back that you are able to plan accordingly. This takes you out of being on the defense when it comes to navigating life changes. By shifting the power in this way, you are now empowered to steer your life change as you see fit.

Now that you know how to set your course, get to work mapping out the first four steps in your journey. If you find yourself needing to complete a different step sooner in order to be set up for later steps, then add it where necessary. This program is all about change. That said you can change your plan at any time you see the need to do so.

# MASTERING CHANGE: NAVIGATION MAP

Create a detailed plan of the next four actions you will take to move your plan forward.

## Action Steps:

Change/Goal: _____ Completion Date: _____

**Action Step 1** _____

Timeline _____

Resources Needed _____

Anticipated Issues _____

**Action Step 2** _____

Timeline _____

Resources Needed _____

Anticipated Issues _____

**Action Step 3** _____

Timeline _____

Resources Needed _____

Anticipated Issues _____

**Action Step 4** _____

Timeline _____

Resources Needed _____

Anticipated Issues _____

While there will be many action steps in your journey, staying focused on small segments at a time will keep your challenges more manageable. As with the *Energy and Focus* exercise, your brain only has a certain capacity for attention. Breaking down the actions needed to make change happen allow for you to focus your energy on what needs to be done in the near future while keeping your task list from overwhelming you.

You will continue to work through your map, continually coming back to review where you are before setting out to undertake the next few steps. As you get further down the road, you will continue to build on the steps you have taken while determining the best course of action to take you the next four steps closer to your goal.

As you complete the first four steps on your *Navigation Map*, take a break to evaluate your progress and make any necessary adjustments going forward. This process is covered in depth as the last step in the *Mastering Life Changes Program*. After evaluating and evolving your plan, print up a new form with the next four steps in your journey. Continue in this way, evaluating every four steps, or more often if needed. This will keep you building on your momentum while constantly adjusting to the changing atmosphere and your growing skill set.

So in this way you will continue towards your goal. Four steps at a time, revisiting your process often, then planning out the next four steps in your journey. Each piece of your map taking you closer and closer to your goal.

*"When we are no longer able to change a situation we are challenged to change ourselves."*

~Viktor Frankl

# Getting Past Roadblocks

It was time for me to move out. But where to? Keeping up with the finances of one household was daunting enough. How would I afford to pay for my wife and kids to stay in their home, while also funding a place for myself? I was out of money, with no idea of where I would live or how I would pay for it. I had just hit a roadblock.

So what would I do now? Staying in the family home wasn't an option. Taking money out of the regular budget would not work. I had to find a place to live and a way to pay for it. I had to walk through the process below for myself.

The reason you list anticipated issues in your map is not to pretend to know everything that could possibly lie ahead. It is to prepare your mind to understand setbacks as part of the process. By expecting obstacles to arise, you remove the emotion of surprise when you encounter them. It allows you to simply say: *Well, I expected something to come up, I guess this is it.*

By the time you get to this step, you are well on your way to owning your life changes. If change is a constant, then even as you set a plan in place to manage change, you have to expect that adjustments will need to be made along the way.

With my roadblock, I needed to take stock of every possible resource available. This is how I developed the first *Assets and Resources Worksheet*. In my case, it was done on the fly. Where could I stay? How would I make more money? Who could help me in any way?

The answers came as I began to focus on what I had to work with rather than what I did not have. I had family and friends with spare rooms. I owned a car. I would have extra time on my hands in the evenings, no longer coming home to family. Resources were available to me which I had not previously needed to use in this way.

Relying on my resources meant staying with family while I got settled and using my car and extra time to earn money as a rideshare driver. This money would then be used to pay for a room to rent.

But let's use a lighter example, let's say you want to attend a concert featuring your all-time favorite artist. This is the big event you have waited for all year. They are finally in your town. You purchased tickets months in advance, planned out the night with your friends, and now you are ready to enjoy the evening. But just after dinner, as you head towards the venue, a noise can be heard rattling in the engine, and you are forced to pull over.

You have just encountered a roadblock. So, what will you do? Will you miss the event? Chances are, your mind will immediately step into the role of working out the contingency plan for getting you to the place you want to be.

In situations like this, the course seems obvious, instinctive if you will. You may already be thinking through several ways you could solve this problem. When your motivation is high enough, and your confidence is healthy, you solve problems without giving it a second thought.

It is when motivation lacks to keep moving forward and you lose confidence in your ability to navigate these obstacles that it becomes easy to give up. Though, to say you gave up or stopped trying is not the cool thing to do. Admitting this to be the case takes hard self-reflection and honest acceptance of the fact that it is in your power to choose whether to fight your way forward or skip town.

It is easier to find blame in the circumstances. This is when many people accept excuses for lack of success. Excuses get reinforced with justifications by reasoning the right thing was done in the face of challenges. *What reasonable person would be expected to make it past these challenges?* It is true, most people would not expect you to push forward. You can find acceptance in the companionship of most people who did not make it beyond a few setbacks.

But I challenge you to ask yourself if you really want to be living the life of *most people.* Is that not in fact why you are working so hard on mastering your life changes right now: so you can enjoy the life most people will not. You are not *most people.* You are better than that. You deserve better than that. Getting past roadblocks is where you separate the *you* from the *most.*

So the first thing you must do when it comes to getting past roadblocks is to accept with full conviction that continuing to move forward and navigating a course through stormy waters is entirely your choice. You must take ownership of the choice you make to move forward or give up, especially when the times get tough.

The reason you don't get to the concert is not that your car broke down. It's not because there was a roadblock. It's because you gave up. It's because you stopped trying.

An important note to make about roadblocks is this: while you do not know which obstacles you will encounter, you know you will encounter some. The good news is that you can plan as best as possible to guide your way past these setbacks when they arise. This is why you list anticipated issues as you plan the course for your map.

Stepping in with the mindset to expect an obstacle, helps to reduce the emotional reaction when you encounter a setback. Instead of reacting to things not going to plan, you can work on the process to get back on track. Possibly even chart a new course altogether. This process is outlined in the *Getting Past Roadblocks Worksheet* on page 126.

## Roadblock

So just how will you get past this roadblock and on your way to that concert? First, you need to clearly define the challenge you are facing. Take some time to think through what is getting in the way of your success. In the concert example, the roadblock is car problems.

Labeling the issue helps to focus your mind on the problem at hand. To say the roadblock is *that you can't get to the concert* is overlooking the cause of the problem and accepting only one possibility as the outcome. That type of thinking is what you say when you are ready to give up. This roadblock is simply that you are having car problems. At this stage, you still have the power to control the results.

## Issues

Each individual setback you encounter creates a different set of issues. One obstacle may produce more than one issue to deal with. If your car breaks down on the way to a concert, you may have to deal with finding new transportation to the concert, as well as getting your car off the side of the road.

Some issues will be urgent and need immediate attention. While other issues can be dealt with later. Sorting out what the issues are, and identifying the urgency around each separate issue helps prioritize where to spend your focus and attention. Those which are less urgent can be pushed to the bottom of your *Focus Triangle* on page 75, while the urgent issues can take the prime space at the top of your mind.

In the *Issues* section, list each of the issues you foresee arising from the current roadblock. Assign an urgency to each issue. Your list may look something like this:

| Issue | Urgency |
|---|---|
| Lacking transportation to the concert | Immediate |
| Car cannot stay on the side of the road | Today- by end of night |
| Car needs to be repaired for future use | Future- by end of week |

As you create a list of the potential issues arising from one hurdle, you may find each issue creates a new roadblock to overcome. This is often the case. Do not allow the issues arising from your setback to keep you from moving forward.

Some of these issues warrant being dealt with as their own separate roadblock. At this point, you simply start this exercise again with the new issue as the roadblock you are focusing on. In this way, you will find the tools and resources needed to work past it.

*Who can help me get past this roadblock?*

Your community and support network are here to help. You have identified who most of these people are when working through your *External Assets & Resources Worksheet* on page 96. Start with this list to get ideas of who you can rely on.

Enlisting support to get past roadblocks requires a two-pronged approach. First, look through your previous lists to determine who can help. Then take a moment to reflect on any additional people who may be valuable for your cause.

For example, your friends accompanying you to the concert might not have been on the initial list of those who could help in a life change, however, each of them has their own support networks. Someone might be able to figure out a ride to the concert while you work on getting your car towed.

Reflect on these questions as you formulate your answer:

- Which new connections have I made since I started this journey?
- Who is most available to help at this moment?

- Who might I need to introduce myself to in order to ask for assistance?
- Which of my friends has connections who might be able to help?

Your community continues to evolve as you work your way through life. Some people will be more prevalent during different parts of the journey. Recognizing this will keep your mind open to finding help beyond your group of close friends.

*What is the worst case if I do not get past this?*

Asking yourself this question allows you to put your situation in perspective. Many times, things are not as bad as you think. Worst-case scenario, you miss a concert and need to replace your car. While missing a concert is disappointing, replacing a car may create challenges or even hardships. But even this is a manageable roadblock.

As you consider your worst-case scenario, reflect on these questions:

- Can I afford the results of the worst-case scenario?
- Can I accept the worst possible outcome?
- If I cannot accept the worst-case scenario, what consequences might occur?
- What benefits could come from allowing the worst-case scenario to play out?

Of course, not all of your issues will be as light-hearted as getting to a concert. While getting past my roadblock to find affordable options for new lodging, I realized my worst-case scenario was that I could be sleeping on the couch at a friend or family member's house. If I could not accept this as the worst-case scenario, I might be on the street sleeping in my car.

Accepting the worst possible outcome allowed my mind to focus on the bigger picture: move life forward and find long-term sustainable housing. Asking the questions will keep you from expending energy and emotions into issues which have little long-term impact on your life. This approach allows you to prioritize when to let things go, and when to give them the full-court press.

*When does this need to be resolved?*

Each issue within the roadblock may have its own timeline. To make it to the concert, you need a ride immediately. Your car may need to be removed from the side of the road within twenty-four hours. But when do you need your car to be working again? This answer will depend on your need for transportation. If you can take a bus to work, you might be able to get by longer without the car.

Consider how long you can live with the status quo. Look through your budget to see if you will be spending money in new ways while you work past this hurdle. If so, how long can you support these expenses? Might you be saving money in other areas? If you now need to buy a bus pass, are you saving money on gas and parking fees? Determining when you need to complete this stage dictates the urgency of finding a resolution.

- How long can I live with the status quo?
- When will I run out of funds if I do not make it past this roadblock?
- What benefits will come from rushing past this obstacle?
- What deadlines will be missed while I work through the situation?

Many factors play into whether or not to push forward or slow down to get around a roadblock. While you will not have a chart to reference filled with the answers for every possibility, you can identify the questions to ask in order to make the best decision case by case. Consider all of the variables when determining the urgency of getting past your roadblock.

*Where might a detour take me instead?*

Life's greatest opportunities often present themselves along the paths you do not expect to take. Just as setbacks can catch you off guard as you travel life's journey, so can favorable circumstances. If you are not keeping your eyes and mind open to the possibilities, they will float past without notice.

As you encounter a roadblock, charting a new course to your destination may be required. As you consider the changes you will make, ask yourself these questions:

- Who might I meet along the way?
- What new opportunities could these connections create?
- Which experiences would I not have had without taking this detour?
- What benefit has been brought to my attention as a result of being set off course?

By keeping an open mind, you are prepared to accept opportunities as they present themselves. Let go of the need to stick to the plan at all costs. This will allow you to find value in the unexpected events as they arise.

*Why did I encounter this roadblock?*

While asking this question may not help in the moment, it can shed an important light on how you got here. This is key to growing as a person and continuing to master the changes ahead. Understanding why you are where you are elevates your skills from getting through change to mastering change.

Asking this question is important in order to keep yourself from making the same mistakes. It keeps you aware of your surroundings as you step into future situations. Being more aware, you will have the opportunity to eliminate potential roadblocks further down the road. Or at least reduce them to speedbumps.

Consider the following questions:

- Were there warning signs which I ignored?
- What issues might have predicted this situation?
- Which habits have I allowed to run on auto-pilot?
- What patterns can be seen in this and previous roadblocks I have encountered?

- What quality checks can I put in place going forward?

Regardless of the current situation, there is plenty to learn. Learning is where the growth comes into play. As I stated at the beginning of this book, you cannot change without growth. Growth comes through the lessons learned along the way. The biggest and most powerful lessons typically present themselves when things do not go to plan. This is when you are tested. This is when you learn the most.

*Resources to tap into:*

As with your connections, you have resources available. Review both your *Internal* and *External Assets & Resources Worksheets* on pages 91 and 96, and make a list of everything that could help you get through this step. As you work through your worksheets, consider the recent changes to your situation which allow for new resources.

A few questions to ask yourself are:

- Which resources will be useful?
- What new resources have become available since I first worked through my *Assets & Resources Assessment*?
- How can I utilize these resources best?
- Which additional resources might I need to source?
- Where can I find additional resources?

By understanding what you have to work with, you can let go of some of the stress of getting through the obstacles. Approaching roadblocks systematically will help you make logical choices to navigate your way past them. By focusing on resources at hand, you reduce the emotion from panic and fear. Staying focused on what you have to work with keeps the power in your hands.

Now, fill out the worksheet on the following page:

# MASTERING CHANGE: GETTING PAST ROADBLOCKS

Roadblocks and setbacks are going to occur. When this happens, refer to your original assets and resources to gather the support needed to keep moving forward.

## Getting Past Roadblocks:

Roadblock _____

Issue _____ Urgency _____

Issue _____ Urgency _____

Issue _____ Urgency _____

Who can help me get past this roadblock?

_____

What is the worst case if I do not get past this?

_____

When does this need to be resolved by?

_____

Where might a detour take me instead?

_____

Why did I encounter this roadblock?

_____

Resources to tap into:

_____

_____

Roadblocks will kick you when you are down. They will catch you off guard. They will test you when you are at your most vulnerable. But you are ready to take them on. You have a community of support and resources at the ready. You have planned as best you can to be ready for the attack.

Learning to take control of the situation and use your resources to chart your way past obstacles is where the power comes in. It is not by never encountering issues that you become strong and powerful, it is through your ability to overcome adversity. As the saying goes, that which doesn't kill you makes you stronger. Each challenge you face builds your muscles and your resiliency.

Challenges, detours, and roadblocks are going to happen. One thing is certain: you will never know how to get past a roadblock if you stop every time you encounter one. Getting past them is what will separate you from everyone else. Getting past roadblocks will open the door to living your best life.

*"Education is the most powerful weapon which you can use to change the world."*

~Nelson Mandela

# Evaluate & Evolve

It's time to take a look at how your plan is going and make adjustments to either stay on track or change course. This is the part of the program called *Evaluate and Evolve.*

Though this is discussed last, you will need to do it all along the way as you work through each *Action Step* in your plan. Whether you are in the middle of your *Navigation Map*, facing a road block, or you have worked your way to the end of your original plan, you need to constantly evaluate your position and evolve as needed.

This step, needs to be layered in at every point along the way. Once you have identified your goal, you may find it needs more clarification or refining. After you have worked through each aspect of your budget, you will need to make adjustments based on changing demands for time or new financial needs that arise. And there is no doubt an evaluation needs to happen in order to assess your situation when you run into roadblocks.

Each of these scenarios has you in the throes of reevaluating your original plan and evolving to meet the current needs.

Let's say, in the very best, albeit unrealistic circumstances, your budget was on track, your plan was perfectly executed, and you did not run into any obstacles through the entire process. If this were the case, you would be standing at your destination wondering what's next. You would still need to evaluate what the next steps should be.

Change is constant. When you have made it to the end of your change or realized your dream, you will need to evaluate and evolve as you move onto the next area of focus in your life.

If your change was relocating, the next step may be to organize your closets or find ways to become involved in your new community. If you were going through a career change and have landed that new job, your next evolution might be to continue training in your new role or set yourself up for a promotion. If your goal was to open a restaurant, you need to now focus on how to grow and sustain your business.

Change never stops. Even when you feel you have successfully navigated the biggest and hardest changes in your life, the simple reward is that you get to determine how to use this new position to best tackle the next stage of changes you will face.

Understanding that the end goal is not to tackle a change and be done with it, but rather to master the process of change so you can steer your changes in the direction you prefer is the key to your success. If you expect to manage one change and then not need to use these tools anymore, you will be disappointed. As we discussed earlier, a major component of your success is your ability to manage your expectations in this area.

This is where the idea of life being about the journey, not the destination, comes true. If you learn to appreciate the journey and master the art of planning your voyage, you become the captain of your vessel. You give up the notion that future happiness is purely based on the outcomes of change. You stop waiting for happiness to arrive once you are in a certain place, but rather, you find happiness at points along the way.

Doesn't this sound like a better option? Why wait for potential happiness when you can enjoy life now?

To work through this step, you will complete the *Evaluate and Evolve Worksheets* on pages 137 and 143. These worksheets will guide you through a series of questions to determine what areas you are satisfied with and in what areas you may need to make adjustments to your plan.

## Evaluate Worksheet

The first page is the *Evaluate Worksheet* which focuses on your status, what you have done, and your satisfaction level. You must first reflect on these aspects of your situation before you can determine where adjustments should be made. Costly choices might be made without considering your circumstances if you make alterations to your goal or your plan without taking this step.

### What is my current status?

Start by listing your current status. Your current status may be something clear and to the point such as: *I have achieved my goal and am ready to evolve to the next level.* Or perhaps you are at some point along the way: *I have made it through my first few steps and need to regroup.* Maybe you are in a place you never anticipated being: *I found a new opportunity while working my way past a roadblock and am reworking my entire plan.*

Answering this question is designed to give you a gauge as to the level of evaluation and perhaps evolution that needs to happen. If you are in the earlier stages of your process you are positioned better to make adjustments which will have time to make bigger impacts on your plan. If you are close to the end of your original plan, you will have had more events happen along the way which will have forced adjustments and evolutions.

Once you determine your status, you will consider what you have gained along the way before deciding your level of satisfaction. Only then can you dig deeper into what changes might need to be made to your plan.

*What lessons have I learned so far in this process?*

Regardless of how far you have come in the process, you have inevitably learned a lesson or two. Lessons come in every shape and size. Many times, the lessons learned from your experiences are the only payoff you get. However, these are priceless when you learn to watch for them and use them to your advantage in the rest of your endeavors.

So what have you learned so far? You may have learned through a success you have had: *Now I know what works for me.* Or perhaps, which is often the case, you learned from a setback: *Now I know what not to do.* Maybe your lesson was how to get started on this very process. Either way, you have more wisdom now than when you started this leg of your journey.

Your lessons may be about yourself, about others, or about the process you are working through. Whatever they are, celebrate them as a win. By recognizing the lessons learned along the way, you are teaching your brain to see the process of mastering change as a winning experience, even in the times when the change does not go as planned.

*What skills have I developed along the way?*

You started this process with a unique skill set which has been developed over your lifetime based on the combination of experiences only you have had. These skills determine which parts of this process are easier for you and which are more challenging. As you work through each step of the *Mastering Life Changes System* you will push yourself in new ways. You will need to focus your attention in ways you might not have otherwise done.

These experiences will develop new skills for you. In combination with the lessons you have learned, you will take these skills into the rest of your life. Look through the stages of your change plan which you have already completed. As you reflect on what you have accomplished so far, make note of all the skills used along the way.

Next look over your list of the skills you have used and circle any that you have not used in the past. Then take another look through your list and circle any skills which you have 'upped your game' in your ability to use. These are the skills you have developed along the way. Just as with the lessons you have learned, you are already coming ahead in life just by having these new skills in your arsenal.

As you identify any new skills, be sure to go back and add them to your initial *Internal Assets and Resources Worksheet* on page 91 in order to keep track of everything you have at your disposal for mastering your life changes.

### Who are the connections I have developed?

As we discussed previously, one of your greatest resources is the community you surround yourself with. Through the experiences of your change, you are likely encountering new people. Or perhaps you are engaging people you already know, but in a new way. This can happen as you open up and share your change journey with others.

When I first came out as gay, I was surprised by the support I had from certain friends with whom I had not been very close. Many of them I would have even considered more acquaintances than friends. As they learned about me, some of them even shared their experiences about having close friends or family members who are also gay.

By sharing the change I was going through, they learned more about me, and how they could support my cause. This brought us closer together. I found allies in people I knew, but did not initially count as resources to rely on for support. Now they are among my closest friends. Though they were not new connections, they were connections I was able to see in a different light and rely on in ways I had not expected.

Some people will come in and out of your life as soon as the need to work together is over. Others will stay with you long term. Both may be potential resources when help is needed. When answering this question, make note of any new connections you have made, or have seen in a different light. I cannot say enough that your community is one of your biggest resources.

If you find connections who were not already listed on your previous *External Assets and Resources Worksheet* on page 96, add them now. Keeping this worksheet up to date will prove valuable as you will rely on it for future steps in your journey.

### *What changes have occurred with my available resources?*

As time passes many changes to your situation develop along the way. With these changes comes access to different resources. Perhaps you did not have a car when you started this journey and now you do. Maybe you sold an asset and now have money to work with. Or perhaps you are working less hours at work and have more time available.

In some cases this will be trading one resource for another: *I am working less hours so I have more time but less money.* Other times you may have found a way to tap into a resource you were not previously relying on: *I refinanced my home in order to have cash for my project.* In some cases you may have made choices to free up the resources you need: *I gave up my club membership so I could have the money and time to apply to my dream.*

However your resources have changed, they will continue to do so throughout your plan and your life. Look back at both the *Internal* and *External Resources Worksheets* on pages 91 and 96. As you review your resource lists, ask yourself: What resources do I have now which I did not previously? Also be honest about which resources are no longer available for you to use.

While answering this question on the upcoming worksheet, also update your initial *Assets and Resources Worksheets* to reflect the changes in your situation. Keeping these current will help you as you refer back to them to get through upcoming steps in your journey, as well as navigating around roadblocks.

*What is my current satisfaction level?*

Whether or not you have completed your original goal, you will have varying levels of satisfaction. You may have arrived at your goal, yet feel unsettled or not satisfied with the result. Perhaps the view from the top is not quite what you expected.

Remember to give yourself credit for the accomplishments which were not part of your initial plan. These could be unexpected opportunities that rose along the way. Or perhaps roadblocks you needed to navigate your way past.

Being satisfied is not a given just because you were successful in achieving your plan. This is exactly why the step to evaluate and evolve is a critical part of the process. If you are satisfied with where this change has brought you, then you can move on to charting the next few steps in your journey, or perhaps get started on your next goal altogether.

If however, you find you have made it through your original plan only to feel let down with the reward, then your next course of action will need to be designed to produce better results. Perhaps even including a way to set yourself up to better manage your expectation of the results.

You may also find yourself in a position where you have not completed your original goal. Maybe not even close. Yet, this does not mean you are not satisfied with the results. You may be completely happy with the way you handled the obstacles you've encountered. You may find you have learned more than expected. Perhaps you even threw your original plan out in favor of a new course which presented itself along the way.

Whatever your level of satisfaction is, it need not be tied to whether or not you have completed your goal. Accepting this fact will open up doors for you as you let go of the traditional thinking that personal satisfaction must be tied to tangible success. The end goal in this entire process is your happiness after all. And your happiness need not be contained to one formula.

*Evaluate Worksheet*

Now, with your questions in mind and your dream waiting for you, work through the *Evaluate Worksheet* on the upcoming page:

# MASTERING CHANGE: EVALUATE & EVOLVE

Through the process you follow to navigate change, you need to check in to see where to adjust and where to stay the course.

## Evaluate:

What is my current status?

_____

_____

What lessons have I learned so far in this process?

_____

_____

What skills have I developed along the way?

_____

_____

Who are the connections I have developed?

_____

_____

What changes have occurred with my available resources?

_____

_____

What is my current satisfaction level?

_____

_____

# Evolve Worksheet

Now that you have answered the *Evaluate* questions you will move on to the next section, the *Evolve Worksheet.* This page is centered on the actions you can take to improve your goal and your plan.

## What needs are not being met by my current plan?

When you started this process and identified your goal, you set out with a plan to ensure certain needs would be met. However, as you progress forward and consider the changes in your situation, the question begs asking: Will my current plan satisfy those needs?

With new resources potentially available, you may also have additional responsibilities. These must be accounted for in your plan going forward. Did your schedule change, requiring you to spend more time at work? Have there been any changes in life such as a new baby, which requires more of your time at home? Are you getting burned out trying to push your dream forward while keeping up with responsibilities?

Any of these scenarios result in you having needs which are not being met. While you focus on moving your dream forward, the rest of your life can be thrown off balance. Asking this question as part of your evaluation, keeps life in balance. This keeps you from taking two steps forward in one area of your life, only to find out that you have completely fallen apart everywhere else.

## How can my current goal be improved upon?

Improving upon your goal does not mean arbitrarily raising the bar. It means adjusting your goal in a way that gives you the best possible outcome. This is a common misconception when asked how you can improve your goal. It could be that you aimed too low and now know your dream can be much bigger than you ever thought possible. Or it could be that you have learned more about yourself and your goal as you started this process. Leaving you realizing your goal as you originally envisioned no longer fits with your ideals. Or perhaps other goals need to be accomplished before focusing on this one.

Improving your goal means that you are adjusting it in any way, bigger or smaller, sooner or later, or changing direction entirely. All with the purpose to have you satisfied with where you end up once you make it to the end of the journey. Perhaps you need to scale down your goal: *I had planned to open a restaurant but a food truck will fit better with my lifestyle and budget.* Maybe your plans were too small: *I planned to move across town but now realize moving across the country is the change I need.* Or perhaps there is a small change to your plan: *I am still going to get a dog, but I will be happier with a lapdog than the big dog I thought I would have.*

Making changes to your goal are perfectly acceptable to do. Staying flexible and open-minded will keep you available for new opportunities and a happier life. Being flexible is one thing, giving up or taking the easy road is another thing entirely.

As you make adjustments to your goal, you must ask yourself why you are making the change you have in mind. If the answer is that you will be in a better place, then yes, you should make the adjustments. If however, your answer is that you are tired of the work or it will be easier to aim lower, then you should not be changing your goal.

Before you adjust your goal, ask yourself this question: When I achieve this goal, will I be satisfied with the changes? In many cases the easier route could be more satisfying: *It was easier to open a food truck and it fits my lifestyle so much better.* But not always: *I opened a food truck instead of a restaurant and now I still crave having my own diner.* Whatever choice you decide, you must be honest with yourself about the reason behind the change.

## What adjustments should be made to my plan?

Whether you have made a big adjustment to your goal, a small tweak, or no change at all, you need to review the course you have prepared to see if any alterations should be made in the way you get there. Even if you have not moved the target for your final destination, your current circumstances could warrant modifications to your next steps.

When considering what adjustments to make, take a look back at the changes you identified in the previous questions on the *Evaluate* portion of this exercise. Do you have more money to work with now? Do you have less time available in your weekly budget? Are new resources available to speed-up a few of the upcoming *Action Steps?* Each change in your situation presents an opportunity to adjust the course towards your best desired outcome.

Perhaps you have hit a roadblock: *I need to pause while I work through the process to get past this.* Or an unexpected opportunity arose: *I need to pursue this before the chance is gone.* You do not always need to make alterations, but asking if you should and considering where they need to be made will keep your plan current with the rest of the changes in your life.

### When is it appropriate to make changes?

Identifying a course of action and implementing it are two different things. They sometimes work one right after the other but that is not always the case. You might have experienced times in your past where you have seen changes need to be made and jumped into action. However there are many times when it took months or even years to implement the actions necessary to make the changes a reality.

This can be the case in times when obstacles are in your way which need to be navigated past before you can shift direction. Or perhaps in times when it is not feasible to adjust your plan until you complete your current course of action. Think of moving on to college from high school: you know you will be making a change, but you cannot start your college career until you have completed high school.

In this way, you must ask yourself when it is right to make the changes you desire to your current plan. A much needed evolution may be obvious in order to reach your dream. But when is the right time to make that adjustment? Is it after a certain step is completed? Or maybe a date you set as a deadline based on other events you need to take into consideration.

Whatever the right timing turns out to be, acknowledge it and write it into your plan going forward. Finding a place for adjustments to fit in will lessen your desire to prematurely jump into action in a reactive way. This will also help you be prepared for future actions as you move your goal forward.

### Who will be affected by these adjustments?

Just as making changes in your life will affect more than just you, so will making adjustments to your plan. When considering shifting course, you must account for people around you. In particular, those to whom you have made promises and commitments based on the original plan.

Yes, this is your plan, and you need to make the choices which are best for you. Yet considering whom those choices will have an impact on and communicating changes with them will keep people on your side. Others have made adjustments and gone out of their way to help you. If you drop your plans, they will wonder why they bothered to invest their time in you. They may feel disregarded or that their time has been wasted.

Keep people on your team by showing appreciation and understanding of how your decisions affect them. A simple acknowledgment of the time they put in while making them aware of your choice will save you from awkward conversations down the road. Instead of having to answer that question of: *Whatever came of all the work we did?* You can take ownership and control of the conversation with a simple, yet important statement: *I appreciate all of the help you have given me, however I have found that it is crucial for me to move in a new direction.*

Acknowledging someone in this way tells them a few things. First it shows that you value their friendship by your willingness to have the conversation. It also relays your appreciation for what they have done for you so far. You will also demonstrate respect for their time and talents by calling out your thanks. The final message this sends is a reassurance that you are not reacting on a whim, or giving up on your

147

dream. You have simply made a choice based on a new understanding of your situation.

You are not giving up your power by understanding and acknowledging the people these adjustments affect. In fact, you gain powerful support by your acknowledgement of those people.

*What is the most important adjustment that needs to be made?*

Your *Navigation Map* might need an overhaul. Or it may require little to no change at all. Either way, it is time for you to get back to action. As you reflect on the questions in this chapter, review the alterations you have decided to make to your plan. With those in mind, ask yourself which one change is the most important.

In other words, if you could only make one change to your plan, what would it be? This question is important in order to bring focus to prioritizing the adjustments you may make. You might be left feeling a bit overwhelmed after evaluating each aspect of your plan and looking at all the ways you could enhance it. Find the one thing that is most worth doing, and focus on that change. If you are not sure which item that is, ask yourself which adjustment will have the biggest impact on your ability to reach your goal.

Directing your focus in this way removes the clutter. It brings your mind back to a state or being ready to take action. This will get you back into your plan and onto your next *Action Step,* renewed and ready to keep moving step by step towards your goal.

*Evolve Worksheet*

With these thoughts in mind, complete the worksheet on the following page:

# MASTERING CHANGE: EVALUATE & EVOLVE

Through the process you follow to navigate change, you need to check in to see where to adjust and where to stay the course.

## Evolve:

What needs are not being met by my current plan?

_____

_____

How can my current goal be improved upon?

_____

_____

What adjustments should be made to my plan?

_____

_____

When is it appropriate to make changes?

_____

_____

Who will be affected by these adjustments?

_____

_____

What is the most important adjustment that needs to be made?

_____

_____

Change is constant. As soon as you get through one step of your process, it is already time to see if your plan itself may need to be changed. This can feel like there is no winning, like things will never be good enough. When you make a plan and it doesn't work out, is that not a failure? Absolutely not.

Making adjustments is not a failure. Having a plan not work out does not mean you did not succeed. In fact the opposite is true: your success comes through your ability to identify those things which are working well and those which need to be changed.

It is not through staying the same that anyone finds success or happiness. It is through growth and growth cannot happen without change. As you work through your process and realize your goals, look for the opportunities to grow, look for the opportunities to change. Look for the opportunities to evaluate and evolve.

Receive free print-friendly versions of all forms and worksheets in this program by visiting awkwardcareer.com/change

*"Without change, something sleeps inside us, and seldom awakens. The sleeper must awaken."*

~Frank Herbert

# Conclusion

So you have reached the end of the book. But the exciting part is that you are at the beginning of the next chapter in your life. A chapter filled with more change, as with the past, but this time you are the author of your own success.

You now have the tools to take control of the situation, to bring yourself back to the shore when you are swimming in an ocean of change. Once there, you can work step-by-step through this process to master the changes in your life.

You could set this book aside and add it to the list of the many books you have read to improve your life. Yet, if you do that, you will have missed the point entirely. This book is not meant to be closed, but rather, to stay open next to you as you work through each change in your life.

Come back to this book as often as you need to. Use it as a reference and a guide as you embark on new adventures and set new goals. This book is here to help, but the magic happens by how you choose to use the information.

You will find that with each new change you encounter in life, this book will find new meaning. An aspect of the process which you relied on less in the past may suddenly become more critical to your success. While others may fade in relevance.

Use the resources beyond this book. Download new copies of the program worksheets at awkwardcareer.com/change as often as you need in order to make the most of every change you encounter in life.

Above all else, remember that change is a catalyst for growth. You will have some changes that are natural and feel great, while others will require all of your energy to make them a success. How you handle change will determine that outcome.

Change in and of itself will always be a part of life. It is not bad, it is not always good. It just is.

## About the Author

Andy Vargo is no stranger to change!

If you ever feel awkward about yourself, then you can understand how Andy Vargo lived the first forty years of his life.  Coming out of the closet at forty doesn't define him, pursuing his passion to help others does. Having changed everything about his life, Andy leads others as a motivational speaker and helps people live their fullest lives as a life coach. At night you can find him working stages around the northwest as a comedian making light of his journey with the gift of laughter.

Awkward is not only his brand, but his style as Andy encourages us all to 'Own Your Awkward' and be true to your genuine self.

Andy hosts the podcast, *Own Your Awkward*, authored the Awkward Journal series, and shares his thoughts and ideas in his blog and video series available at awkwardcareer.com.

# Also Available by Andy

Choose the sixty-day guided journal that is right for the net part of your journey.